OECD Development Co-operation Peer Reviews: Belgium 2015

This work is published under the responsibility of the Secretary-General of the OECD. The opinions expressed and arguments employed herein do not necessarily reflect the official views of OECD member countries.

This document and any map included herein are without prejudice to the status of or sovereignty over any territory, to the delimitation of international frontiers and boundaries and to the name of any territory, city or area.

Please cite this publication as:
OECD (2015), *OECD Development Co-operation Peer Reviews: Belgium 2015*, OECD Publishing, Paris.
http://dx.doi.org/10.1787/9789264239906-en

ISBN 978-92-64-23985-2 (print)
ISBN 978-92-64-23990-6 (PDF)

Series: OECD Development Co-operation Peer Reviews
ISSN 2309-7124 (print)
ISSN 2309-7132 (online)

The statistical data for Israel are supplied by and under the responsibility of the relevant Israeli authorities. The use of such data by the OECD is without prejudice to the status of the Golan Heights, East Jerusalem and Israeli settlements in the West Bank under the terms of international law.

Corrigenda to OECD publications may be found on line at: *www.oecd.org/about/publishing/corrigenda.htm*.

Conducting the peer review

The OECD's Development Assistance Committee (DAC) conducts periodic reviews of the individual development co-operation efforts of DAC members. The policies and programmes of each member are critically examined approximately once every four or five years. Five members are examined annually. The OECD's Development Co-operation Directorate provides analytical support, and develops and maintains, in close consultation with the Committee, the methodology and analytical framework – known as the Reference Guide – within which the peer reviews are undertaken.

The objectives of DAC peer reviews are to improve the quality and effectiveness of development co-operation policies and systems, and to promote good development partnerships for better impact on poverty reduction and sustainable development in developing countries. DAC peer reviews assess the performance of a given member, not just that of its development co-operation agency, and examine both policy and implementation. They take an integrated, system-wide perspective on the development co-operation and humanitarian assistance activities of the member under review.

The peer review is prepared by a team, consisting of representatives of the Secretariat working with officials from two DAC members who are designated as "examiners". The country under review provides a memorandum setting out the main developments in its policies and programmes. Then the Secretariat and the examiners visit the capital to interview officials, parliamentarians, as well as civil society and NGO representatives of the donor country to obtain a first-hand insight into current issues surrounding the development co-operation efforts of the member concerned. Field visits assess how members are implementing the major DAC policies, principles and concerns, and review operations in recipient countries, particularly with regard to poverty reduction, sustainability, gender equality and other aspects of participatory development, and local aid co-ordination. During the field visit, the team meets with representatives of the partner country's administration, parliamentarians, civil society and other development partners.

The Secretariat then prepares a draft report on the member's development co-operation which is the basis for the DAC review meeting at the OECD. At this meeting senior officials from the member under review respond to questions formulated by the Committee in association with the examiners.

This review contains the Main Findings and Recommendations of the Development Assistance Committee and the report of the Secretariat. It was prepared with examiners from Finland and Italy for the Peer Review of 17 June 2015.

Table of Contents

Tables

Figures

Boxes

Abbreviations and acronyms

ACROPOLIS	Academic Research Groups for Policy
B-FAST	Belgian First Aid and Support Team
BFFS	Belgian Fund for Food Security
BIO	Belgium Investment Company for Developing Countries
BTC	Belgian Technical Cooperation
CNCD	National centre for development Cooperation
COORMULTI	Co-ordination of multilateral issues
CSO	Civil society organisation
DAC	Development Assistance Committee
DGD	Directorate-General for Development Cooperation and Humanitarian Aid
DGE	Directorate-General for European Affairs and Cooperation
DGM	Directorate-General for Globalisation and Multilateral Affairs
EU	European Union
FPS	Federal Public Service
FPS FA	Federal Public Service, Foreign Affairs, Foreign Trade and Development Cooperation
GDP	Gross domestic product
GNI	Gross national income
ICP	Indicative Cooperation Programme
LDC	Least developed countries
NGA	Non-governmental actor
NGO	Non-governmental organisation
ODA	Official development assistance
OECD	Organisation for Economic Co-operation and Development
PCD	Policy coherence for development
TDC	Trade for Development Center
UN	United Nations
WBI	Wallonia-Brussels International

Signs used:

EUR	Euros
USD	United States dollars
( )	Secretariat estimate in whole or part
-	Nil
0.0	Negligible
..	Not available
...	Not available separately, but included in total
n.a.	Non applicable

Slight discrepancies in totals are due to rounding.

Annual average exchange rates (EUR for USD) were:

2009	2010	2011	2012	2013
0.7181	0.7550	0.7192	0.7780	0.7532

Belgium's aid at a glance

BELGIUM

Gross Bilateral ODA, 2012-13 average, unless otherwise shown

Net ODA	2012	2013	2014[a]	Change 2013/14
Current (USD m)	2 315	2 300	2 385	3.7%
Constant (2013 USD m)	2 427	2 300	2 374	3.3%
In Euro (million)	1 801	1 732	1 797	3.8%
ODA/GNI	0.47%	0.45%	0.45%	
Bilateral share	62%	57%	59%	

a. Preliminary figures.

Top Ten Recipients of Gross ODA (USD million)	
1 Democratic Republic of the Congo	138
2 Côte d'Ivoire	138
3 Burundi	61
4 Rwanda	51
5 West Bank and Gaza Strip	33
6 Viet Nam	29
7 Benin	25
8 Mali	23
9 Niger	21
10 Mozambique	21
Memo: Share of gross bilateral ODA	
Top 5 recipients	30%
Top 10 recipients	38%
Top 20 recipients	50%

By Income Group (USD m)

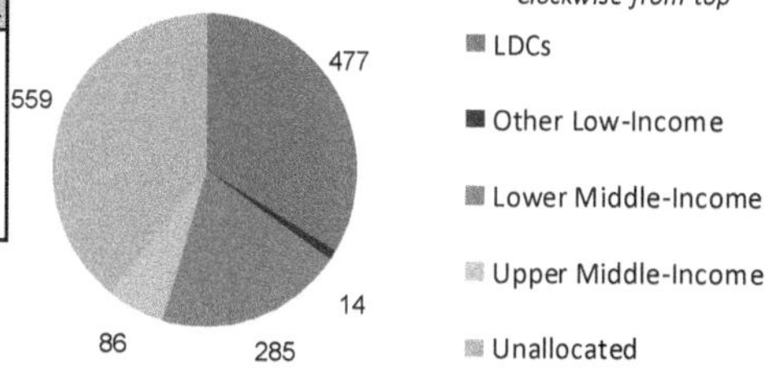

477
559
14
86
285
Clockwise from top
LDCs
Other Low-Income
Lower Middle-Income
Upper Middle-Income
Unallocated

By Region (USD m)

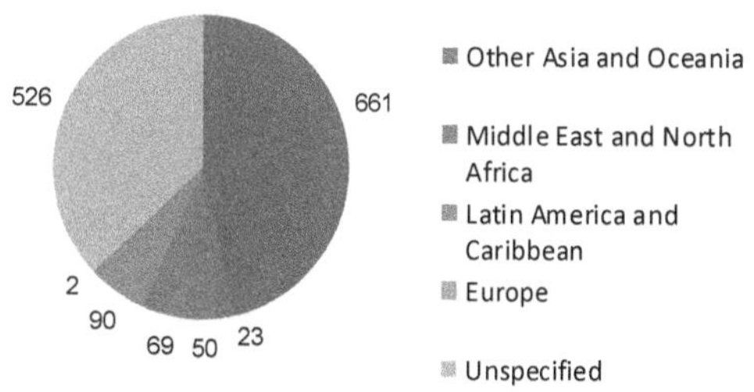

526
661
2
90
69
50
23
South of Sahara
South & Central Asia
Other Asia and Oceania
Middle East and North Africa
Latin America and Caribbean
Europe
Unspecified

By Sector

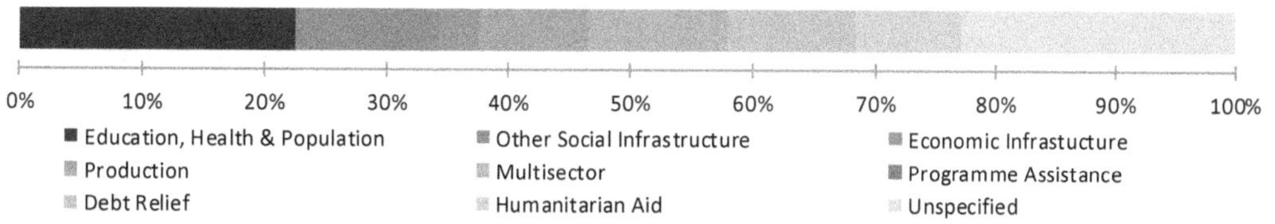

0%
10%
20%
30%
40%
50%
60%
70%
80%
90%
100%
Education, Health & Population
Other Social Infrastructure
Economic Infrastucture
Production
Multisector
Programme Assistance
Debt Relief
Humanitarian Aid
Unspecified

Source: OECD - DAC ; www.oecd.org/dac/stats

Figure 0.1 Implementation of Peer Review Recommendations from 2010

Not Examined: 1 (6%)
Not implemented: 2 (12%)
Implemented: 9 (53%)
Partially: 5 (29%)

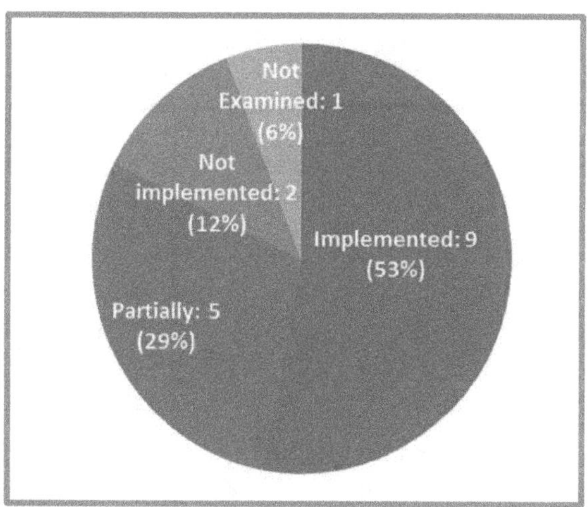

Context of Belgium's peer review

Context

Belgium is a federal state with a population of 11 million. Since October 2014, it has been governed by a coalition formed by four political parties, including liberals, Christian democrats and Flemish nationalists.

The Belgian economy is very open and highly integrated into the major European economies represented by France, Germany, the Netherlands and the United Kingdom. According to the OECD, economic activity in Belgium withstood the financial crisis relatively well and has been growing since early 2013. Nevertheless, recovery remains fragile. Economic growth will remain moderate as a result of weak economic activity in the European Union and feeble domestic demand, which is due in part to fiscal consolidation (OECD, 2015).

Belgium performs well in terms of the numerous criteria in the OECD's Better Life Index. In 2014, it ranked above the average for the 36 OECD countries for the dimensions of work-life balance, income and wealth, housing, civic engagement, education and skills. However, it was below average for environmental quality and personal security.

The priorities for the new federal government include balancing the national budget by 2018 and increasing employment and competitiveness. Significant cuts have been made to government spending, which also affect development co-operation – the subject of the present report.

Sources:

EIU, "Belgium", December 2014, Economist Intelligence Unit, London.

OECD (2015), *OECD Economic Surveys: Belgium 2015,* OECD Publishing, Paris, http://dx.doi.org/ 10.1787/eco_surveys-bel-2015-en.

OECD (2014), *How's Life in Belgium? OECD Better Life Initiative,* www.oecd.org/statistics/BLI%202014%20Belgium%20country%20report.pdf.

FPS FA (2014a), *Examen par les pairs de la Belgique 2015 - Mémorandum*, [OECD DAC Peer Review of Belgium: Memorandum], Federal Public Service, Foreign Affairs, Foreign Trade and Development Cooperation, Brussels.

The DAC's main findings and recommendations

1 Towards a comprehensive Belgian development effort

Indicator: The member has a broad, strategic approach to development and financing for development beyond aid. This is reflected in overall policies, co-ordination within its government system and operations

Main Findings

Belgium is strategic in the way it promotes sustainable development beyond its aid programme. It is firmly committed to an inclusive, international regulatory environment, which it sees as central to finding solutions to global public risks. The government advocates for peace and security, forgotten crises, aid orphans, and least developed countries in the European Union (EU) and internationally. It participates actively in the debate on the post-2015 agenda, and its new environment strategy focuses on global public goods.

In EU budget negotiations, for example, Belgium argued for a fragility indicator in DEVCO's model for allocating resources. With a high share of its official development assistance (ODA) going to least developed countries it leads by example in pushing the international community to meet the UN target for aid going to these countries, which is 0.15-0.20% of GNI.

At home, Belgium has put in place the legal and policy foundations for taking forward its commitment to ensure that its domestic policies are development-friendly. This is in line with the 2010 peer review recommendation. Policy coherence for development is now rooted in the 2013 Federal Law on Belgian co-operation and humanitarian aid.

Setting up the institutions to ensure that policies support sustainable development rather than undermine it, takes time, however. Key challenges include getting cross-government buy-in and commitment, identifying and agreeing on priority issues and a plan for addressing them, and ensuring that mechanisms for institutional co-ordination – whether new or existing – address and arbitrate on policies through the lens of development. A major challenge is to mobilise federal ministries and strengthen their capacity to assess the impact of domestic policies on development.

Belgium's Regions and Communities have their own approach to policy coherence for development. Going forward, the May 2014 joint statement by the federal government and the governments of the Communities and Regions represents an important step for co-ordinating positions: the signatories committed to consider development issues in all policies, to co-ordinate the federal, inter-federal and European level, and to consider the impact of decisions in the areas of environment, agriculture, economy, trade, finance, migration, security and energy on international development goals.

In addition, Belgium's rich pool of researchers and civil society actors can play their part by providing good analysis of issues of incoherence. Indeed, the 2014 Royal Decree on the interdepartmental committee encourages NGOs to bring evidence of the benefits of coherence into development co-operation strategies.

Belgium has been reinforcing its approach to leveraging ODA and other instruments to increase private investment for development – particularly for the local private sector in developing countries. A number of official instruments have been developed. Some of these are in the form of tied aid or are oriented towards export promotion. The Belgian Investment Company for Developing Countries (BIO), which focuses on supporting local private sector companies, is particularly promising.

Now that BIO has signed a management contract with the Belgian State and has strengthened its role as an official development co-operation actor, there is even greater scope to increase private financing in favour of development. BIO is putting in place a monitoring and evaluation mechanism in order to assess the impact of its investments on development. More systematic co-ordination, as planned, between Belgian public and private actors that support local private sector development can also contribute to synergies and increase coherence between activities in partner countries.

Recommendations

1.1 Now that the foundations are in place for making its policies more coherent, Belgium should develop a plan of action on a few policy issues of strategic priority which it can influence and be pragmatic in how it uses institutional mechanisms.

1.2 Belgium should further strengthen the development impact of BIO's investments and should ensure that its other official instruments for leveraging private investments for developing countries also contribute to sustainable development.

2 Belgium's vision and policies for development co-operation

Indicator: Clear political directives, policies and strategies shape the member's development co-operation and are in line with international commitments and guidance

Main Findings

Set out in its 2013 Federal Law for Development Cooperation, Belgium's clear overall vision is "contributing to sustainable human development". The new law has widespread support and ownership: a range of actors were engaged in the three-year process it took to update it, and some of their policy priorities were taken on board. While the law does not apply to federated entities, it is consistent with their priorities.

Belgium has made several important advances with its policy and strategic framework since 2010, which are in line with the peer review recommendations. For example:

- The law is more comprehensive by including both development and humanitarian assistance. It also addresses how Belgium will support private sector development in developing countries.
- New sector and thematic strategy papers are more practical. Prepared in close consultation with Belgian staff in partner countries, NGOs and the research community, these strategies build on evidence from the ground and partners' experience.
- The new strategy on situations of fragility is pragmatic, proposing practical tools for programming and is a useful guide for all Belgian actors on how to engage in fragile contexts.
- Finally, the 2011 multilateral strategy gives high priority to making this support effective. Belgium's policy of paying multiyear core contributions to multilateral partners increases predictability while also reducing administrative costs – an approach that is highly valued by its partners.

At the same time, the government has committed to new strategic improvements which, if implemented, could change the face of Belgian development co-operation. To increase the scale, impact and quality of its programmes and partnerships, the Directorate-General for Development Cooperation (DGD) will channel a higher share of its aid to least developed countries (LDCs) and fragile situations. It will also work with fewer partnerships whether multilateral, NGO or developing countries.

In May 2015, the government reduced the number of partner countries for its government-to-government co-operation from 18 to 14, of which 12 are LDCs and 8 are countries in fragile situations. It will also phase out governmental co-operation with six middle income countries over the coming four years. Conscious that exiting from long-standing partner countries needs to be managed carefully, Belgium's robust new strategy for middle income countries notes that its relationship with these countries will evolve – rather than end – in order to respond better to specific needs. As it phases out of governmental development co-operation in these countries, Belgium could usefully learn from the experiences and evaluations of other DAC members.

The poverty reduction focus of Belgium's development co-operation is reflected, in particular, by its support to LDCs and fragile situations. While Belgium does not have specific policy guidance on poverty reduction, it states that it will focus on inclusive economic growth that eradicates poverty, exclusion and inequalities. Given the multiplicity of thematic and sector priorities outlined in Belgium's law, policies and strategies, there is a risk of diluting the focus on poverty reduction.

Environmental issues seem to be better integrated into Belgium's development co-operation than gender equality and women's empowerment. The comprehensive – and ambitious – environment strategy is supported, for example, by toolkits and training developed by the research platform on climate and the environment (KLIMOS) as well as the ACROPOLIS initiative. The DGD plans to update the 2002 strategy note on gender, which can be informed by the findings and recommendations of the recent evaluation of gender and development.

Recommendations

2.1 To demonstrate how its development co-operation addresses the needs of poor people, as intended by its policy commitments, Belgium should develop practical guidance and promote monitoring and evaluation of poverty impacts.

2.2 Belgium should match its commitment to mainstreaming gender equality and women's empowerment with the leadership, capacity and tools needed to make this happen in practice.

3 Allocating Belgium's official development assistance

Indicator: The member's international and national commitments drive aid volume and allocations

Main Findings

Belgium has enshrined in law its commitment to providing 0.7% of its gross national income (GNI) as official development assistance. Yet its aid has declined substantially since 2010 when it reached a peak of USD 3 billion, the equivalent of 0.64% of national income. In 2014, Belgian ODA was USD 2.4 billion and 0.45% of GNI. While this ratio is higher than the DAC average of 0.29%, it is set to decrease to 0.38% by 2019 following the significant cuts approved by the government in the 2015 budget – about EUR 750 million compared to the multiannual projections in 2014. On this basis, Belgium will not deliver on its aid commitment in the medium term.

These cutbacks, like those incurred in other DAC member states, take place in a context of the governments' commitment to decrease budget deficits. At the same time, the drop in the aid budget undermines the credibility of Belgium's commitments and its reputation just as the international community is negotiating the post 2015 development framework and as DAC members face increasing international pressure to deliver on their aid promises. The Belgian government has yet to signal when the aid budget could return to growth and produce a plan for reaching 0.7%.

While the budgetary outlook is negative, the clarity of the savings that need to be made by 2019 has increased overall aid predictability. At the same time, DGD faces the challenging task of applying the cuts in reality. While it has some lead-in time since the real cutbacks to the programme will start only in 2017, its key partners face high uncertainty about future support and need to plan for possible cutbacks.

All budget lines – multilateral, non-governmental, humanitarian and government-to-government – will be cut. At the same time, the strategy and criteria the Directorate-General will use to make the cuts need to be coherent with the government's decision to increase the focus of the programme by reducing the number of partners and increasing synergies between the various budget lines.

DAC data show that bilateral allocations focus strongly on Africa and LDCs with 70% of total ODA going to sub-Saharan Africa in 2013. This is in line with Belgium's priorities. In addition, Belgium provided 0.16% of its GNI to LDCs in 2013 meeting the UN ODA target for LDCs of allocating 0.15-0.20% of gross national income. Support to fragile states seems low, however, given Belgium's stated focus on them: it reached USD 465 million in 2013 accounting for 34% of total bilateral ODA. Nevertheless, in 2014 the Directorate-General allocated 62% of its budget for governmental co-operation to these states.

The priority Belgium gives to multilateral co-operation is also evident in its aid allocations: between 2008 and 2013 an average of 38% of its ODA was allocated to multilateral organisations and a further 13% as multi-bilateral.

Sectoral priorities are less evident in allocations, notably the productive sectors and, within them, agriculture. However, according to DGD, Belgium is close to achieving its target of investing 15% of total ODA in agriculture – it was 13.4% in 2013.

Belgium has not set deadlines for achieving its targets of allocating 50% of total ODA to LDCs and 0.25% of its gross national income, which goes beyond the UN LDC target of 0.15 0.20%. To make good on its promise, it will need to allocate more of its aid to these countries, but it is not yet clear how it will do this. While the new list of partner countries for governmental co-operation focuses on LDCs, Belgium's country programmable aid is quite low – in 2013 it was 28% compared to the DAC average of 54.5%. Twenty-five per cent of bilateral aid is core support to NGOs, while humanitarian aid, refugee costs and imputed student costs combined account for about another quarter of bilateral aid.

Recommendations

3.1 To meet its international commitments, Belgium should reverse the decline of its ODA and start planning for increasing it in order to deliver on its commitment to 0.7%.

3.2 Belgium should ensure that its strategy and the criteria it uses for applying the budgetary cuts between 2017 and 2019 will enable it to deliver on its geographical and sectoral commitments. It should communicate actively with key partners about its strategy.

3.3 Belgium should set deadlines for achieving its targets for increasing its total ODA to LDCs through the different channels of its aid programme.

Managing Belgium's development co-operation

Indicator: The member's approach to how it organises and manages its development co-operation is fit for purpose

Main findings

Since the 2010 peer review, Belgium has reinforced the leadership and management of its institutional system for development co-operation, making it more strategic and taking steps towards delivering more co-ordinated and high quality development co-operation.

In particular, the Directorate-General for Development Cooperation at the Ministry of Foreign Affairs, Trade and Development, which manages at least 60% of the aid budget, is in a stronger position to steer the system strategically. The strategic management committee now approves policies and strategies before they are submitted to the Minister for Development Cooperation.

The Director-General's 2013-19 management plan provides a clear vision of how business processes will need to evolve to ensure that Belgian development co-operation is fit for purpose. Strategic objectives address, for example, the need to invest in expertise, to optimise co-ordination between different parts of the system and ensure that DGD has more efficient processes, a stronger results focus, quality assurance and risk management.

The new and updated management contracts with the main implementing agencies, the Belgium Technical Cooperation (BTC) and the Belgian Investment Company clarify roles and responsibilities in relation to DGD in line with 2010 peer review recommendation. In addition, exchange of information between the federal government and regions has improved thanks to regular (bi-annual) meetings.

Nevertheless, DGD and BTC recognise that they need to continue to adapt organisational structures and their business models in order to remain relevant in the changing landscape of development co-operation and to evolve with the needs of developing countries. In particular, there are questions around the degree to which development co-operation will be integrated with foreign policy, and how the current approach to delivering government-to-government co-operation, including through technical co-operation, should evolve.

By delegating more financial and programming authority to the field, the DGD and the Agency would be more capable of engaging in policy dialogue and co-ordination with the government and other partners, while also being better placed to assess contextual and programmatic risks and to identify and respond flexibly to evolving demands and needs. For example, as Belgium scales up its involvement in fragile states, it will need to ensure that it has the right resources, including sufficient delegated authority, so that programmes can be effective in these rapidly changing environments. BTC's recent review of its organisational model in the Democratic Republic of Congo could serve as a basis for adjusting its programming structures in other countries.

The previous peer review had identified human resource management as a major challenge, particularly within the Ministry of Foreign Affairs. Little progress has been made since then, and the Ministry has yet to find an effective way to have a critical mass of development expertise in the right places – headquarters and field. Staffing levels are set to decrease further in the Ministry: while in 2014 DGD had 150 headquarter staff and 73 attachés in embassies, 61 staff will retire by 2019. Also, current rules impede internal career staff from gaining crucial development experience in the field. At the same time, BTC has good expertise and a strong presence on the ground, although the majority of its staff are employed in projects co-managed with the partner government.

Finally, while DGD has an annual staff training plan and BTC gives high priority to training and staff development, resources are constrained in both organisations. As seen in Rwanda, demand for training from field-based staff is high.

Recommendations

4.1 Building on recent reforms, Belgium should ensure that its business models for development co-operation are capable of adapting and responding to the evolving priorities and needs of developing countries, especially LDCs and countries in fragile situations, and the changing global context.

4.2 Belgium should ensure that its approaches to managing and delivering development co-operation match the human resources available across the development co-operation system so that the right staff and capacities are deployed to the right places.

5 Belgium's development co-operation delivery and partnerships

Indicator: The member's approach to how it delivers its programme leads to quality assistance in partner countries, maximising the impact of its support, as defined in Busan

Main findings

Belgium has been working on several fronts to advance with its commitments to deliver quality assistance and to maximise the impact of its ODA as defined in the Busan Partnership for Effective Development Co-operation.

A keen supporter of EU joint programming, it has put this priority in law and supports EU processes in partner countries. Belgium is valued for its open, dynamic, pragmatic and constructive ways of engaging and co-ordinating with other donors. It is also leading in the area of statebuilding, using country systems where possible as seen by its support to education in Burundi.

The government's commitment to have projects fully executed by partners and to use country systems in a more differentiated way can increase alignment as well as partner country ownership. Moreover, an increasing share of Belgian ODA is untied – 98.1% was untied in 2013 compared to 96.5% in 2012.

Belgium's budgeting process enables it to provide multiyear predictability to most of its partners. Governmental co-operation, which accounted for 25% of DGD's aid budget in 2014, is fully negotiated with partner countries and the priorities set out in the *programme indicatif de coopération* (PIC) respond to partners' demands. In Rwanda, for example, Belgium invests in the government's priority sectors and abides by its division of labour. It also takes a programmatic approach in the health sector where it provides budget support. At the same time, the bulk of the programme is delivered through co-managed projects.

However, Belgium still needs to increase the predictability of its disbursements, which is undermined by significant delays in committing the overall indicative budget to programmes and projects. According to DGD, its new programming guidelines address this challenge: projects will be identified before the country programme is approved. In addition, BTC will have more freedom to modify project outputs and activities to a changing environment without approval from headquarters. It is too soon to tell if the changes will increase timeliness and relevance. Communicating the new procedures to partners will be important so that they understand their role and how they should contribute, and to manage expectations.

While DGD is planning to use risk analysis more systematically for planning and programming, it is doing this in a political context of limited risk tolerance. As a result, it is hard to get the balance right between taking risks to seize development opportunities and avoiding risk. It could also stifle DGD's and BTC's ability to innovate with new ways of delivering development co-operation.

There have been moves towards greater whole-of-government consultation in Brussels (e.g. monthly meetings for the Sahel and the bi-monthly meetings on Central Africa). However, these efforts have not led to a common Belgian position towards its fragile partners or clear roles and responsibilities for who will do what across government. This is a missed opportunity to bring foreign policy tools together to support a more effective response. There could also be a more strategic regional approach with closer co-operation between embassies in priority regions, as found in Rwanda.

DGD hopes to generate greater synergies between the mix of instruments and range of partners that channel its ODA to partner countries. Current plans to develop more integrated country strategies have the potential to increase the impact and the visibility of the totality of Belgium's aid. However, convincing governmental and non-governmental actors to buy into this new approach is challenging and strong political support will be crucial for success.

Finally, while non-governmental actors are major partners for delivering Belgian ODA, DGD does not have a clear policy setting out the objectives, rationale, added value and approaches to partnering with civil society. Having such a policy could help guide important reforms that aim to reduce transaction costs. It would also provide a solid basis for allocating the budget for non-governmental actors and enhancing the focus on results, while also supporting the enabling environment for civil society in partner countries, as agreed in Busan.

Recommendations

5.1 Belgium should speed up programming processes and increase flexibility to use and adjust aid instruments to the context.

5.2 A clear policy should guide partnerships with civil society organisations.

5.3 To support a more effective response in fragile situations Belgium should define a context-specific whole-of-government position with clear roles and responsibilities for who will do what.

6 Results management and accountability of Belgium's development co-operation

Indicator: The member plans and manages for results, learning, transparency and accountability

Main findings

Managing for development results has become a high priority for Belgian development co-operation which has taken a range of measures since the last peer review to strengthen the results focus of its programme, to enable it to learn from results monitoring, and be more accountable for results.

Conscious that there is not yet a strong results culture in Belgian development co-operation and that there is a weak understanding of key concepts in the ministry and partner organisations, the consultative approach taken to develop the strategic note on "Results and Development" has helped to generate a common vision for results.

The results strategy also aims to build a system that shows how Belgium contributes to partner countries' results, which is in line with the Busan commitment. While the Directorate-General for Development Cooperation must ensure that partners have results-based management systems, it also relies on its partners to assess and report on the performance of Belgian aid. Ensuring that they focus on results that meet developing countries' priorities, assess performance on the basis of these priorities, and draw on partner countries' data and systems will be a challenge. This is less of a challenge at the project level where BTC agrees results matrices with the partner government – BTC's challenge is measuring development outcomes.

Belgium's evaluation system is in line with DAC evaluation principles: the 2013 Law on Development Cooperation distinguishes between internal evaluations and the external evaluations conducted by the independent evaluation service, which has a clear evaluation policy that focuses on evaluating results.

To increase evaluation capacity, the Law requires that the evaluation systems of Belgian development actors, including NGOs, be certified according to international evaluation standards. The Special Evaluation Service is mandated to certify the organisations. This can be time and resource intensive. Given cutbacks to the Service's budget and staffing, Belgium needs to ensure that the Office of the Special Evaluator can fulfil its whole mandate.

As a next step, Belgium should ensure that evaluations are used more systematically as management tools and feed into institutional learning. A number of thematic evaluations have led to the reformulation of strategic notes. At the same time, some management responses do not appear to be playing their role as a feedback mechanism that ensures follow-up to recommendations.

DGD's objective to become a knowledge centre for development co-operation is timely: it needs to build an effective knowledge sharing system in a context where staff levels are decreasing and fewer staff have experience from the field.

In 2014, Belgium published for the first time aid information according to the common standard. It has also invested in developing its own online database (ODA.be). However, it is unlikely to meet the 2015 deadline for publishing timely, comprehensive and forward-looking information. Moreover, with only a few members of staff managing statistics and reporting, it has limited capacity, at present, for maintaining a high-quality database over the long term. It also needs to develop capacity to analyse the data in a way that the information the system generates feeds into decision making and enables greater accountability to partners as well as Belgian taxpayers.

DGD and BTC work strategically and closely with Belgian non-governmental actors to build public awareness and support for development co-operation. Belgium's strong commitment to this is evident in Article 7 of the 2013 Law, the relatively high budget for these activities as well as the priority given to having an evidence base for communication and development education strategies. There is scope, however, for Belgium to communicate more comprehensively about results and risks in development co-operation.

Recommendations

6.1 Belgium should ensure that its new system for managing for development results is capable of drawing together reporting by implementing partners so that it can assess performance, be accountable for development outcomes while also being useful for decision making.

6.2 The Office of the Special Evaluator and DGD should have an effective mechanism for ensuring that there is appropriate follow-up and implementation of evaluation findings and recommendations.

6.3 DGD should transform its existing approach to managing information into an effective knowledge sharing system which learns from results and evidence for forward-looking planning.

7 Belgium's Humanitarian assistance

Indicator: The member contributes to minimising impact of shocks and crises; and saves lives, alleviates suffering and maintains human dignity in crisis and disaster settings

Main findings

Belgium has made enormous progress on its strategic approach to humanitarian assistance over the last four years, modernising its legal, policy and budgetary framework to allow for quality, predicable funding arrangements in areas where it can clearly add value. There is also now a clear policy focus for the humanitarian programme linked to Belgium's overall strategic priorities.

There are new tools to deliver on the new strategic framework. Funding allocations – set out, and thus ring-fenced for four years, in the budget – heavily favour core funding to the multilateral system and pooled funds, meaning that Belgium's focus is actually on specific partnerships, rather than on specific crises and themes. This is a useful strategy, providing predictability and flexibility for partners, mitigating against the potential for politicised decision making, and providing an efficient way to disburse, given the limited number of humanitarian staff in DGD. It has also helped provide the basis for quality partnerships with multilateral agencies.

The humanitarian team is usefully plugged into cross-government mechanisms on protracted crises and emergency situations, allowing them to influence Belgium's overall policy and operations. This has also helped increase awareness of humanitarian principles in different ministries.

The new framework allows for holistic programming, enlarging the scope of programming to include areas such as recovery and risk reduction. However, links between the development and humanitarian programmes are not being strengthened. Instead Belgium uses humanitarian funds for rehabilitation and recovery activities. Belgium now needs to determine how it will make use of these new opportunities – particularly on risk reduction – perhaps through including risk elements in development partner country strategies.

The budget volume is sufficient to meet Belgium's humanitarian objectives, although it will, in line with wider fiscal consolidation measures, decline by 25% over the next five years.

Disbursement has been an issue in the past, mostly due to government administrative procedures outside DGD's control. This has led to underspending. DGD needs put in place measures to prevent this from happening in the future.

Even though staff numbers have been cut, the humanitarian team believes it is still able to manage the humanitarian portfolio effectively, especially now that the emphasis is on large strategic partnerships rather than small high workload grants. However, there is little time left over for strategic reflection, or for input to thematic debates at global level.

The previous peer review asked Belgium to focus more on monitoring results – of itself as a donor and of partners. There has been some progress on this as part of the overall management plan. However, it is still not entirely clear how Belgium assesses its progress or results. For NGO grants in particular, there seems to be a strong focus on fiduciary risk over and above attention to results and learning.

Indeed, there is not yet a quality relationship with NGOs, who were consulted on the overall strategic approach, but they were not engaged in dialogue on strategy or programming in 2014, and had unclear guidance on how to apply for funds. The dialogue was launched again in 2015.

Investments in pooled funding mechanisms are set to rise from 39% of the budget (2015) to 50% (2019). However, Belgium does not yet engage on the boards of these pooled funds, limiting opportunities to add value to this part of the portfolio.

Recommendations

7.1 Belgium should review its strategy for engaging with NGOs in humanitarian assistance, to ensure that it is getting the most value out of these partnerships. As part of this, Belgium is encouraged to finalise guidance for NGOs seeking to access project funding.

7.2 Belgium should clarify how it is going to add value to its significant investments in pooled funding mechanisms – perhaps by involving itself more in the governance arrangements of these funds, either directly or by working through other donors.

Secretariat's report

Chapter 1: Towards a comprehensive Belgian development effort

Global development issues

Belgium is a strong advocate for the preservation of global public goods. It does this mainly through the European Union (EU), by participating in international security treaties and international organisations. It helps put forgotten crises and conflicts on the EU agenda and takes part in military training and operations under the Common Security and Defence Policy.

Belgium is particularly committed to resolving forgotten crises and conflicts

As a member of numerous international organisations and with an involvement in many parts of the globe, Belgium actively promotes a fairer, more prosperous world in key policy areas such as peace and security, human rights and the rule of law. It believes that the shared challenges facing our planet can only be solved through global regulation, and puts particular emphasis on the decision-making role of the European Union (EU), lobbying hard so that forgotten crises and ongoing conflicts are on the EU agenda. For example, during EU budget negotiations, Belgium argued for an indicator on the amount of aid for countries with situations of fragility. The country is also notable for its adherence to international security treaties (CGD, 2014) and has taken part in various military training missions and operations under the Common Security and Defence Policy.

Belgium is playing an active role in international discussions on the post-2015 framework for sustainable development. Its new environmental strategy is set in the context of securing global public goods (DGD, 2014a).

Policy coherence for development

Indicator: Domestic policies support or do not harm developing countries

Despite some progress, delivering on its commitment to make its policies development-friendly remains a challenge for Belgium. Policy coherence for development (PCD) is rooted in the new federal law on Belgian co-operation and humanitarian aid, and is supported by a joint declaration common to both the federal and federated governments. Belgium has put in place a number of mechanisms which can help take forward its commitment to ensure its policies are coherent with development and many Belgian civil society actors have the capacity to analyse policies for their coherence. On the other hand, interest in and commitment to making policies coherent with development does not seem to pervade all levels of government. In addition, setting-up the institutions for ensuring that policies support sustainable development has fallen behind schedule and priority issues have yet to be identified.

Belgium is firmly committed to policy coherence for development but has yet to identify priority issues

The 2010 OECD-DAC peer review highlighted Belgium's shortcomings in terms of the coherence of policies concerning development and invited it, among other things, to develop an explicit policy statement on policy coherence for development (OECD, 2010). Progress has been made since then, and there are signs that awareness of the importance of this issue is growing at the highest levels of government. For example, policy coherence for development is cited as an objective in the Law on Development Cooperation adopted on 19 March 2013, which "recognises the contribution made by PCD to Belgium's general development objectives and aid effectiveness" (Kingdom of Belgium, 2013). Commitment to PCD is therefore enshrined in Belgian law and policy – the stage is now set for delivering on it.[1]

The regions of Flanders and Wallonia, the Wallonia-Brussels Federation and the Communities have their own approaches to PCD.[2] While the Law on Development Cooperation only applies to the federal government (not to these federated bodies), a declaration issued on 23 May 2014 stated the commitment of the federal government and the governments of the regions and communities to policy coherence for development (Kingdom of Belgium, 2014e). This means Belgium is committed to taking development into account in all policies; to co-ordinate at federal, interfederal and EU level; and to look at the impact on international development goals of decisions affecting the environment, agriculture, the economy, trade, finance, migration, security and energy.

Despite this commitment, Belgium has not identified issues coherence or incoherence that should be addressed as a priority; neither has it defined a plan or milestones for doing this. It is encouraging, however, that the Minister for Cooperation has signalled his intention to establish priorities in the areas set out by the European Union.

Like most DAC members Belgium still has a long way to go to resolve problems of inconsistency in its policies. The Commitment to Development Index 2014 ranks Belgium 16th out of 27 countries (down from 10th in 2013). While it stands out for its low production of fossil fuels and high participation in international security treaties, its total score is weakened by the high level of agricultural subsidies and its arms exports to poor, undemocratic states (CGD, 2014). The OECD working group on bribery, moreover, believes that Belgium does not do enough to combat the bribery of foreign public officials by Belgian citizens and businesses, especially in terms of the limited resources it makes available and the legal framework (lack of) for this purpose (OECD, 2013).

The ambitious institutional set-up is taking time to materialise

Belgium is creating a new institutional set-up for policy coherence for development. This includes several new mechanisms[3] which should enable the country to honour its EU commitments and implement the DAC's recommendation (see Annex A).

In practice, putting such an ambitious set-up in place is complex, and is hindered by bottlenecks between the varying degrees of power at federal and federated entity levels and the latters' preference for using existing structures. For example, the Interministerial Conference has not been created on the grounds that permanent co-ordination bodies already exist. At the same time, it is not clear that these co-ordination bodies actually deal with issues related to coherence or incoherence with development. For example, while COORMULTI[4] and the biannual forum attended by the Directorate-General for Development Cooperation and Humanitarian Aid (DGD) and the administrations of the federated entities dealing with development co-operation[5] bring issues to political attention, no specific institution has been officially designated to monitor and follow up on these issues. Nevertheless, PCD is discussed at meetings of the Federal Public Service (FPS) Foreign Affairs Directorate-General for Coordination and European Affairs to prepare

Belgium's contribution to the European Commission's biannual report on policy coherence for development.

Another key proposed PCD mechanism – the Interdepartmental Committee[6] – has still not been established because some ministries and entities are late in appointing representatives. The "Coherence Unit" that should support this committee is in place, but does not yet have sufficient resources to create the hoped-for momentum. These delays and lack of capacity are regrettable, since the committee could play a key role in preparing issues to be taken up by the Council of Ministers - a relevant forum for debating coherence. Moreover, the Minister for Development Cooperation is a member of the council and is well placed to flag development concerns. The fourth mechanism, - the Advisory body with representatives from NGO platforms and academia - has opted to focus on EU trade, the Great Lakes strategy, preparing Belgian positions at the World Bank and the rights of people and businesses. Whatever the subject, it is important that Advisory body's discussions go beyond finding a coherent policy in general and ensure that they also focus on development.

Federal Public Services are, generally speaking, insufficiently mobilised and do not have the capacity to study the impact of their policies on developing countries. The provision of training in March 2015 on policy coherence for development for "provisionally designated" members of the Interdepartmental Committee is a welcome initiative, although it will take several months before the effects can be measured.

The analysis of regulatory impact on development is of limited use

Since 2014, government bills, draft Royal Decrees and proposals for rulings submitted to the Council of Ministers have been analysed for their coherence with development using a tool known as AIR (analysis of regulatory impact). This analysis flags potential amendments to be made or accompanying measures that could be provided.

While this analysis of regulatory impact is commendable, especially because it promotes transparency, it has limited impact on coherence. There is little room to change course and the exercise has not, as yet, identified regulatory proposals that have more than a marginal impact on developing countries. Furthermore, it does not deal with draft legislation on national security or international treaties, even when they affect development (e.g. taxation, trade, bribery). It is not evident, therefore, that this approach is useful for helping to make Belgian policies and legislation development-friendly.

Belgium has a wealth of NGOs, researchers and academics who regularly flag inconsistencies in Belgian policy. The 2010 peer review recommended harnessing this analytical capacity to track the effects of various policies on development (Annex A). Since then, a Royal Decree has encouraged Belgian NGOs to provide technical support for "the inclusion of PCD in strategy notes by Belgian development co-operation" (Kingdom of Belgium, 2014c). These organisations must nevertheless mobilise efforts to deliver pertinent analysis that can influence government policy.

The delays with the institutional set-up and in setting priorities prevent the government from reporting on progress to the Federal Parliament

The delays in setting up the institutional system for ensuring that policies are supportive of development mean that Belgium is still not ready to report on the progress it has achieved in this area. By law, the annual report on Belgian development co-operation should make PCD recommendations to the Federal Parliament, a task that will fall to the Coherence Unit. In the absence of the Interdepartmental Committee and a list of priority issues, it is hard to imagine a progress report being produced in the near future.

Financing for development

Indicator: The member engages in development finance in addition to ODA

Belgium mobilises financial resources for development in addition to ODA, focusing on investment in the local private sector. There is room to increase the development relevance of some of its instruments.

Belgian ODA supports private sector growth for sustainable human development

Belgium's strategy for mobilising finance for development is to use ODA to catalyse growth in the local private sector in developing countries – specifically small and medium-sized enterprises (DGD, 2013b).[7] This approach was introduced in the Law on Development Cooperation,[8] as well as in Belgium's strategy for local private sector development (DGD, 2013b). Belgium also intends to involve Belgian businesses and investors in development financing (De Croo, 2014). Its strategy for mobilising additional finance for development extends to domestic resource mobilisation earmarked, including tax revenues (*ibid*).

Belgium has tools for mobilising additional finance, mainly in the local private sector

Belgium has a range of instruments for mobilising resources in addition to ODA, mainly through the private sector, but the degree to which this finance spurs development depends on the instrument used.

The instruments for mobilising the local private sector, the biggest of which is the Belgium Investment Company for Developing Countries (BIO)[9], are intended, in theory, to be biased towards development. BIO's investments are designed to have a catalytic effect, allowing beneficiary institutions to attract additional private financing (SES, 2014). While its process for choosing companies and projects in which to invest ensures that they will promote development in theory, BIO must now implement new monitoring procedures to measure development impact in practice. In addition, but on a smaller scale, the Trade for Development Centre provides technical and financial support to producers in priority countries that adhere to sustainable and fair trade practices.[10]

At present, activities supported by Belgian actors targeting the local private sector remain fairly uncoordinated. Now that BIO is part of the Belgian co-operation system (Chapter 4),[11] there is scope to co-ordinate better with the FPS Foreign Affairs. A working group has also been set up to study areas for co-operation between BIO and Belgian Technical Cooperation (BTC). Belgium is planning to create a platform – *entreprendre pour le développement* (enterprise for development) – for a limited number of public and private Belgian organisations involved in developing the local private sector to help promote policy coherence for development. While the initiative has the potential to improve co-ordination and consistency between supported activities, its terms of reference will have to take account of the lessons from the previous platform, created in 2008 and now inactive.

Other instruments for mobilising the Belgian private sector for development fall within the framework of tied aid and are mainly focused on export promotion. Financing granted by FINEXPO[12] doubles the resources available to developing countries to purchase capital goods and services. However, the mechanisms for selecting and monitoring projects do not provide any certainty that these resources actually contribute to development (SES, 2011). Similar questions arise over funding granted by regional export assistance agencies (SOFINEX and Flanders Investment and Trade). Since the federated governments have competence for trade it will be essential to boost synergies and complementarity to ensure the leveraging effect, and, especially, to increase financing for development.

Belgium reports non-ODA flows

Belgium monitors and reports to the DAC on non-ODA resources earmarked for developing countries. These are mainly private capital flows at market conditions. They include:

- private export credits guaranteed or provided by the Export Credit Agency – *Office National du Ducroire* – which amounted to USD 787 million net in 2013 and USD 430 million in 2012
- foreign direct investment, which reached USD 6.397 billion in 2013.

Charitable donations from private sources came to USD 958 million in 2013. Belgium also reports operations financed by BIO under "Other public sector contributions". These came to USD 190 million of gross disbursements in 2013.

Notes

1. The government's policy orientation paper – *Exposé d'orientation politique – coopération au développement* (de Croo, A. 2014) and the Directorate-General for Development Cooperation and Humanitarian Aid's 2013-19 management plan (DGD, 2014b) both argue for the inclusion of development in Belgium's foreign policy and recommend increased intra-governmental co-ordination.

2. The Flemish Region's 2007 framework decree for development co-operation, for example, aims to increase policy coherence for development in the policy areas which fall under the competency of the Flemish Community and Region. The Wallonia-Brussels Council for international co-operation has made PCD a policy priority.

3. These consist of (i) an interministerial conference headed by the Prime Minister; (ii) an interdepartmental committee of Federal ministries, Regions and Communities; (iii) an advisory body, and (iv) a secretariat charged with monitoring these entities.

4. The COORMULTI (i.e. co-ordination of multilateral issues) mobilises the Federal Public Services, Regions and Communities ahead of Belgium's position statements to international bodies. Whether the parties actually attend depends on the subject of the meeting.

5. In March 2015, PCD was formally added to the agenda at the meeting of the forum between DGD and the administrations of the federated entities responsible for development co-operation.

6. The committee will be chaired by the Director General of the Development Cooperation and Humanitarian Aid Directorate of the FPS Foreign Affairs, Foreign Trade and Development Cooperation.

7. This strategy aims to improve the investment climate, promote the development of the local private sector and fair and sustainable trade, and stimulate international trade.

8. The law promotes the role of the private sector in fostering inclusive, sustainable growth to eradicate poverty and achieve sustainable human development.

9. BIO invests through the acquisition of share capital or loans. The deployment of financial resources came to EUR 600 million in 2013.

10. The Trade for Development Centre has a budget of EUR 13 million over four years. Another "enterprise for development" budget line promotes partnerships between entrepreneurs' associations, partner country producers and European associations.

11. Since 2014, relations between BIO and the Belgian State have been governed by a management contract consistent with Belgium's development co-operation objectives and principles.

12. FINEXPO is an interministerial advisory committee managed by the Administration of Foreign Affairs, which aims to reduce or stabilise the financing cost of capital goods and services exports while contributing to the development of the countries that receive the aid. The instruments available to FINEXPO allow aid to be granted within the framework of DAC's arrangements.

Bibliography

Government sources

BIO (2014), *Sustainable Human Development by Strengthening the Private Sector in Developing Countries, Annual Report 2013,* Belgian Investment Company for Developing Countries, Brussels.

BTC (2013), *Dossier technique et financier, Trade for Development Centre 2014-2017,* Belgian Technical Cooperation, Brussels.

BTC (2012), *Les femmes, actrices du commerce équitable,* BTC – Trade for Development, Brussels.

De Croo A. (2014), "Exposé d'orientation politique – Coopération au développement", Minister for Development Cooperation, Digital Agenda, Telecoms and Postal Services, Doc 54 0020/017, 14 November 2014, the Chamber of Representatives, Brussels.

DGD (2014a), *Environment in the Belgian Development Cooperation – Strategy note,* Directorate-General for Development Cooperation and Humanitarian Aid, Brussels.

DGD (2014b), "Plan de management 2013-2019", unpublished document, DGD, Brussels.

DGD (2013a), *La coopération belge au développement dans les pays à revenus intermédiaires – Note stratégique,* March 2013, DGD, Brussels.

DGD (2013b), *La coopération belge au développement et le secteur privé local : le soutien d'un développement humain et durable – Note stratégique,* DGD, Brussels.

DGE Europe (2013), *Annual Report on the Activities of the European Union 2013,* FPS Foreign Affairs, Foreign Trade and Development Cooperation, Brussels.

Federal Public Service Finance (2014), *Finexpo, Rapport annuel 2013,* FPS Foreign Affairs, Foreign Trade and Development Cooperation, Brussels.

Kingdom of Belgium (2014a), *Loi modifiant la loi du 19 mars 2013 relative à la Coopération belge au Développement,* 9 January 2014, Moniteur Belge, Brussels.

Kingdom of Belgium (2014b), *Arrêté royal portant assentiment au 1er contrat de gestion entre l'État belge et la société anonyme de droit public "Société belge d'Investissement pour les Pays en Développement",* 2 April 2014, Moniteur Belge, Brussels.

Kingdom of Belgium (2014c), *Arrêté royal relatif à la création d'une commission interdépartementale sur la cohérence des politiques en faveur du développement,* 2 April 2014, Moniteur Belge, Brussels.

Kingdom of Belgium (2014d), *Convention Générale de Mise en Œuvre Relative au Programme "Trade for Development Centre" 2014-2017,* Brussels.

Kingdom of Belgium (2014e), *Déclaration de l'État fédéral, régions et communautés de la Belgique sur la Cohérence des politiques en faveur du développement,* 23 May 2014, Brussels.

Kingdom of Belgium (2013), *Loi relative à la Coopération au Développement,* 19 March 2013, Moniteur Belge, Brussels.

Kingdom of Belgium (1997), *Loi relative à la coordination de la politique fédérale de développement durable,* 5 May 1997, Moniteur Belge, Brussels.

SES (2014), *Évaluation de terrain des investissements de la Société belge d'investissement pour les pays en développement (BIO),* Special Evaluation Office for Belgian Develpment Cooperation, FPS Foreign Affairs, Foreign Trade and Development Cooperation, Brussels.
http://www.bio-invest.be/fr/news/135-levaluation-sur-le-terrain-des-investissements-de-bio-confirme-leur-pertinence-et-additionalite.html.

SES (2011), *Evaluation of the Belgian Instruments in Support of Foreign Trade Eligible as Official Development Assistance (ODA) - Évaluation Finexpo*, SES, FPS Foreign Affairs, Foreign Trade and Development Cooperation, Brussels.

Other sources

CGD (2014), Belgium, Center for Global Development, www.cgdev.org/page/belgium-6.

CNCD 11.11.11 (2014), *Modernisation ou instrumentalisation de l'aide? Rapport 2014 sur l'aide belge au développement,* National Centre for Development Cooperation, Brussels.

CNCD 11.11.11 (2012), *L'Aide en temps de crises : repli ou coopération ? Rapport annuel 2012*, CNCD, Brussels.

CONCORD (2011), *Country Profile: Belgium in Spotlight on EU Policy Coherence for Development, Report 2011*, European NGO Confederation for Relief and Development (CONCORD), http://tinyurl.com/pgxwnkd.

Eggen, M. and N. Janne d'Othée (2013), "Ceux qui ont faim ont droit - Le droit à l'alimentation comme outil de cohérence des politiques en faveur du développement", *Point Sud* No. 10, October 2013, CNCD-11.11.11, Brussels.

OECD (2014), *Better Policies for Development 2014: Policy Coherence and Illicit Financial Flows,* OECD Publishing, Paris, http://dx.doi.org/10.1787/9789264210325-en.

OECD (2013), *Phase 3 Report on Implementing the OECD Anti-bribery Convention in Belgium*, OECD, Paris.

OECD (2010), *OECD Development Assistance Peer Reviews: Belgium 2010,* OECD Publishing, Paris, http://dx.doi.org/10.1787/9789264098268-en.

Trade Union Development Cooperation Network (2014), *The Private Sector and Its Role in Development: A Trade Union Perspective,* Trade Union Development Cooperation Network, Brussels.

Chapter 2: Belgium's vision and policies for development co-operation

Policies, strategies and commitments

Indicator: A clear policy vision and solid strategies guide the programme

The federal law on Belgian development co-operation sets out Belgium's vision, which is to achieve sustainable human development. There is broad support for this goal. The government has improved its recent strategies, making them more practical and relevant for programming in the field.

The federal law sets out a clear vision for Belgian co-operation and is widely supported

March 2013 saw the adoption of a new federal law on Belgian development co-operation (Kingdom of Belgium, 2013) following a lengthy process of broad consultation that began in 2010 and which gave Belgian civil society organisations the opportunity to put their concerns to the government. Consequently, most actors appear to buy into the objectives and principles of the law.[1]

The law sets out the purpose of Belgian development co-operation, which is to contribute to sustainable human development. Belgium plans to achieve this objective by supporting inclusive economic growth in order to eradicate poverty, exclusion and inequality, and boost its partners' capacity at every level. In addition to introducing policy coherence for development, humanitarian aid and private sector development are also covered by the law. While the law provides a framework for all channels of federal co-operation, it does not apply to federated entities and therefore does not represent a shared vision of development across all Belgium's development actors.[2] At the same time, the policies and priorities of the federated entities do not conflict with the vision embodied in the law.

The previous 1999 law encouraged Belgium to translate its policy priorities into strategic guidance for all sectors and themes defined by the law. While older guidance notes are often theoretical, recent strategies are more practical, setting out priorities, and ways to implement the strategy and find synergies with other federal actors over the medium term. The fact that NGOs and academics helped to produce these strategies should secure additional buy-in. In order to ensure that they are useful for programming, staff and partners responsible for implementing Belgian co-operation should be involved in evaluating them.

Approach to allocating bilateral and multilateral aid

Indicator: The rationale for allocating aid and other resources is clear and evidence-based

Belgium has a legal, strategic and operational framework that clarifies the key principles guiding how it allocates aid. However, the focus is blurred by the large number of objectives and sub-objectives, and the fact that their strategic importance varies between documents. The decision to focus aid on fewer countries and partners, and on a maximum three sectors in partner countries, is in line with objectives to deliver more effective aid. It now falls to the government to clarify the rationale for distributing aid according to its new list of priority countries, to set out a timetable for withdrawal from non-priority countries and regions, and to define the steps leading to the adoption of country strategies. There is also scope to refine the criteria for distributing multilateral aid.

Criteria for allocating bilateral aid geographically are clear; policy objectives are less clear

The new law and related Royal Decrees delineate how Belgium's development co-operation is allocated in terms of countries and themes (Kingdom of Belgium, 2014). The law identified 18 partner countries,[3] selected according to the prevalence of poverty and inequality or on the basis of their fragility, the relative weight of Belgian development co-operation and its comparative current and future advantage.[4] The law also identifies four major areas and five priority themes,[5] while respect for human rights is both an objective and a fundamental principle of Belgian development co-operation.

Taken together, the law, the government's policy declaration on development co-operation (De Croo, 2014), strategic guidance approved since 2013 and DGD's management plan (DGD, 2014a) form the legal, policy and operational framework for Belgian co-operation. This framework features a great many objectives, priorities and secondary objectives, however, which are interchangeable between documents, and make it difficult to discern the government's exact policy.

In an effort to comply with EU development policy (DGD, 2013a)[6] and to bring an end to aid fragmentation, the government decided in May 2015 that it will focus its government-to-government co-operation on 14 partner countries.[7] It is also committed to engage in no more than three sectors in each country. Twelve of the countries in the new list of priority partners are least developed and eight are in situations of fragility. Belgium will phase out governmental co-operation in six middle income countries over the coming four years. The approach to phasing out is guided by the development co-operation law, and when relevant by the strategy for middle-income countries (DGD, 2013).[8] This increasing concentration is laudable. It should help in monitoring activities and managing resources, while also enabling Belgian to scale up its support for greater impact. It also offers an opportunity to clarify the rationale behind aid allocations, to draw up a timetable for withdrawal from countries and regions, and to prepare the various stages leading to new country strategies.

Multilateral co-operation is strategic

Multilateralism is a key instrument of Belgian foreign policy, reflected in the significant resources granted to multilateral institutions (Chapter 3). In line with its goal of more effective aid, the government plans to allocate at least 30% of federal aid to the multilateral channel and to reduce the number of priority partner organisations.

The policy paper on multilateral co-operation (DGD, 2011) defines Belgium's strategy for its major multilateral channels (the United Nations, EU and the international financial institutions). This strategy subscribes to international commitments[9] and the European Commission's Programme for Change. It aims, among other things, to ensure that bilateral and multilateral co-operation are complementary. Belgium's policy of providing multiannual core contributions[10] increases aid predictability and reduces administrative costs – a practice that is appreciated by multilateral organisations.

DGD no longer has a special division for multilateral co-operation: every department manages its own contacts with UN agencies according to the relevant theme (Chapter 4). Multilateral co-operation is now co-ordinated by a new thematic directorate (known as D2; see Annex D). This does not seem to have affected the regularity of Belgian contributions to these bodies. Nevertheless, efforts will need to be made to co-ordinate and follow up on decisions, in particular between DGD and other federal departments.

Belgium uses its network of representatives to multilateral organisations and its membership of specialist donor groups to good effect. Until 2015, when it withdrew its membership, Belgium was also very active in MOPAN (the Multilateral Organisation Performance Assessment Network) drawing on its discussions and recommendations. DGD also plays an advisory role for bodies that represent Belgium in the international financial institutions,[11] and has appointed an advisor to the World Bank's Executive Bureau.

Policy focus

Indicator: Fighting poverty, especially in LDCs and fragile states, is prioritised

Belgium's commitment to poverty reduction and inequality is evident in its firm support for least developed countries (LDCs) and fragile states. While Belgium has no specific policy on poverty reduction, it is addressed to varying degrees in other strategy papers, often in connection with inclusive, equitable and sustainable growth. Belgium has reinforced the link between humanitarian assistance and development co-operation. Its strategy on fragile states and situations is relevant and helpful to officials.

Various strategic documents cite the goal of combating poverty

While there is no specific strategic guidance for combating poverty, exclusion and inequality, poverty reduction is one of the goals enshrined in the Law on Development Cooperation, it is mentioned in various policy documents, and is further fleshed out in recent strategic notes. Belgium's development co-operation also subscribes to the principles, declarations and conventions of the United Nations, including those concerning the environment, human rights and decent work.

Belgium's poverty focus is reflected in its strong commitment to LDCs and fragile states. The new government will target North and West Africa, and the Great Lakes Region, where most countries are least developed, and plans to devote 0.25% of its gross national income (GNI) to this part of the world (DGD, 2014a). Six of Belgium's 18 priority countries (identified in the law) are fragile states. There is a dichotomy, however, between Belgium's declared objectives and the reality of its ODA (Chapter 3).

DGD states that it intends to develop more integrated programmes in its partner countries- especially LDCs and fragile states – to combine poverty reduction and institutional capacity building with efforts on climate change, the environment, peace and security. It will have to ensure, however, that this does not divert its attention away from the imperative to reduce poverty and inequality.

Belgium has reinforced the link between development and humanitarian programmes

Belgium has responded to the 2010 peer review recommendation to strengthen links between relief and development, mostly by expanding the scope of eligible expenditure under the new Royal Decree (Chapter 7). This means that humanitarian funds can now be used for rehabilitation and socio-economic recovery, which is good practice. However, Belgium does not systematically factor the risk of crisis into its programming.

Belgium takes a pragmatic approach to fragile states and situations

Belgium has a new guidance note for fragile situations, focused on statebuilding, and referencing both the Fragile States Principles and the key areas of the New Deal (DGD, 2013; Chapter 5). The guidance is pragmatic, and focused around ten principles, with practical means for programming in fragile contexts. Staff say that the new strategy has increased awareness on how to work in fragile contexts across the Belgian system.

Belgium's commitment to cross-cutting issues could be strengthened

Achieving gender equality and women's rights, as well as the protection of the environment and natural resources, are key priorities of the Law on Development Cooperation. While the government's policy declaration devotes a section to the environment, climate and natural resources, it makes no reference to gender equality and women's rights (de Croo, A, 2014).

Like most DAC members, Belgium aims to incorporate gender into all aspects of development co-operation, and to fund specific activities targeting women. A recent independent assessment of the implementation of Belgium's policy on gender equality, however, reveals that several commendable initiatives are encountering resistance and failing to generate the hoped-for results (SES, 2014). The reasons given include insufficient understanding and acceptance of the gender policy, scarce resources and incentives, and a lack of support from the top. In Rwanda, for example, the lack of clear and operational guidance was one explanation given for why gender equality is not well integrated into all projects (Annex C).

Belgium's approach to gender is defined in the strategy – currently being revised – on the *Equality of rights and opportunity between women and men* (DGD, 2002). It would be advisable for the updated strategy to take account of the recommendations made in the evaluation of how this strategy was implemented (SES, 2014). Belgian Technical Cooperation has developed an ambitious strategy on gender and development (BTC, 2010), but its status and implementation are unclear since it is DGD that is responsible for formulating development co-operation strategies.

One of the main lessons to be learned from experiences across the DAC is that sufficient financial and human resources need to be ring-fenced if cross-cutting issues are to be successfully included in programmes (OECD, 2014). While Belgian co-operation does not have a specific gender budget, it does have gender expertise in FPS Foreign Affairs, in the minister's policy unit, in DGD's thematic division and BTC.[12] However, this does not seem to be sufficient to cover both the policy and operational aspects of governmental co-operation. The new gender strategy that is being prepared and the creation of a gender platform in 2014 are steps in the right direction. These initiatives must be backed up with enough support from senior management to make the cultural shift required for gender equality to be properly embraced by all development co-operation programmes. To achieve this, it will need to develop some incentives, provide better training, and have an action plan to track how the strategy is being implemented.

DGD's strategy on the environment was jointly prepared with the Directorate-General for European Affairs and Cooperation (DGE) and the Directorate-General for Globalisation and Multilateral Affairs (DGM), the relevant federal ministries, research institutes, Belgian universities and other non-governmental actors, BIO and BTC (DGD, 2014b). It focuses on the preservation of global public assets and lists three core issues: (i) the integration of environmental governance within the four basic sectors of Belgian co-operation: education, health, basic infrastructure and agriculture; (ii) specific environmental support for water, the sustainable use of land and soil, forest stewardship and waste management; and (iii) policy coherence for development (DGD, 2014b). Although commendable, these objectives are ambitious and technically and politically complex. Furthermore, links have yet to be established between the overall strategy for Belgian development co-operation, the strategy for middle-income countries – one goal of which is to combat global warming – and BTC's environmental principles (BTC, 2013).

Belgium is one of the DAC members to have effectively integrated biodiversity into development co-operation (Drutschinin et al., 2015), but the lack of a dedicated environmental budget and expertise within BTC could slow implementation. To achieve its goals, DGD is counting on the green "climate" fund; its climate, environment and natural resources department; the KLIMOS platform; and the support of ACROPOLIS, universities and federal scientific establishments. It also intends to draw up an operational plan to implement the strategy and a results tracking chart. These actions that will be vital if the actors involved are to meet the challenges of sustainable development.

Notes

1. While the law was amended on 9 January 2014, its objectives have not been changed (Kingdom of Belgium, 2014).

2. The three federated entities – Flanders, Wallonia-Brussels International and Brussels-Capital – pursue development co-operation activities according to their own principles and priorities. Their ODA represents just 1-2% of Belgian ODA.

3. Over half of these countries appear on the list of least developed countries: Benin, Burundi, Democratic Republic of the Congo, Mali, Mozambique, Niger, Rwanda, Senegal, Tanzania and Uganda. The eight remaining countries are evenly spread between lower-middle-income countries and territories – Bolivia, Morocco, Vietnam, the West Bank and Gaza Strip – and higher-middle-income countries – Algeria, Ecuador, Peru and South Africa.

4. Poverty and inequality are measured according to the level of socio-economic development, the Human Development Index (HDI) adjusted for inequality, and the human poverty index or the country's level of fragility. Two other criteria concern the efforts made by the partner country in pursuit of its socio-economic development and good governance.

5. These four themes are healthcare, agriculture and food safety, training and education, and basic infrastructure. The five priority fields are human rights, including children's rights, decent and permanent work, social consolidation, gender equality, and the preservation of natural resources.

6. The EU is holding talks on the withdrawal of EU aid from a certain number of higher-middle-income countries.

7. The new list of priority countries for governmental co-operation includes: Benin, Burkina Faso, Burundi, Democratic Republic of Congo (DRC), Guinea, Mali, Morocco, Mozambique, Niger, Rwanda, Senegal, Tanzania, Uganda, West Bank and Gaza Strip

8. The exit strategy should be developed "in co-operation with the country concerned and the other donors present in order to carry out the exit within a maximum period of four years".

9. These commitments include the Universal Declaration of Human Rights, the Beijing Conference on Women in 1995, the Millennium Development Goals and the Paris Declaration on Aid Effectiveness.

10. These unearmarked contributions are channelled to partner organisations' general resources every four years. Country programmes sometimes use delegated co-operation to help fund multilateral organisations' projects.

11. The FPS Finance represents Belgium in the international financial institutions.

12. There is one full-time person working on gender in DGD's thematic division, a human resources specialist at the FPS Foreign Affairs and an advisor who tracks the thematic aspects of co-operation, including gender, within the Minister's policy cell. At BTC, a senior expert is responsible for integrating the gender policy into the programmes and gender experts are present in a few partner countries.

Bibliography

Government sources

BTC (2013), *Déclaration environnementale 2013*, Belgian Technical Cooperation, Brussels.

BTC (2010), *Égalité des genres – Notre stratégie 2010-2014*, BTC, Brussels.

De Croo A. (2014), "Exposé d'orientation politique – Coopération au développement", Minister for Development Cooperation, Digital Agenda, Telecoms and Postal Services, Doc 54 0020/017, 14 November 2014, The Chamber of Representatives, Brussels.

DGD (2014a), "Plan de management 2013-2019", unpublished document, Directorate-General for Development Cooperation and Humanitarian Aid, Brussels.

DGD (2014b), "Environment in the Belgian Development Cooperation – Strategy Note", DGD, Brussels.

DGD (2013a), "La coopération belge au développement dans les pays à revenus intermédiaires – Note stratégique", March 2013, DGD, Brussels.

DGD (2013b), "Note stratégique pour les situations de fragilité", April 2013, FPS FA, DGD, Brussels.

DGD (2011), "Note de politique sur la coopération au développement multilatérale, partie I", March 2011, DGD, Brussels.

DGD (2002), "Note stratégique égalité des droits et des chances entre les femmes et les hommes", DGD, Brussels.

FPS FA (2015), *Budget Général des Dépenses 2015*, Federal Public Service, Foreign Affairs, Foreign Trade and Development Cooperation, Brussels.

FPS FA (2014), *Examen par les pairs de la Belgique 2015 - Mémorandum*, [OECD DAC Peer Review of Belgium: Memorandum], FPS FA, Brussels.

Kingdom of Belgium (2014*), Loi modifiant la loi du 19 mars 2013 relative à la Coopération belge au Développement*, 9 January 2014, Moniteur Belge, Brussels.

Kingdom of Belgium (2013*), Loi relative à la Coopération au Développement*, 19 March 2013, Moniteur Belge, Brussels.

SES (2014), *A Difficult Path towards Equality: Gender and Development in Belgian Cooperation*, Service de l'Évaluation spéciale, FPS FA, Brussels.

SES (2013), *How Green is our Development Assistance? Thematic Evaluation of the Belgian Cooperation in the Field of Environment*, SES, FPS FA, Brussels.

Other sources

Drutschinin, A., et al. (2015), "Biodiversity and development co-operation", *OECD Development Co-operation Working Papers*, No. 21, OECD Publishing.

OECD (2014), *Mainstreaming cross-cutting issues: Seven lessons from DAC Peer Reviews*, OECD Publishing, http://dx.doi.org/10.1787/9789264205147-en.

Chapter 3: Allocating Belgium's official development assistance

Overall ODA volume

Indicator: The member makes every effort to meet domestic and international ODA targets

Belgium's ODA budget shrank by 0.20% between 2010 and 2013, and further significant cuts are forecast between 2015 and 2019. It is unlikely it will meet its ODA commitments, including the 0.7% gross national income target which is enshrined in law. Although public opinion and the government are in favour of this target, Belgium does not have a roadmap or timetable for increasing ODA and reaching its target. While the 2015 federal budget clearly sets out the cutbacks that DGD has to make up to 2019, DGD has yet to identify how and where it will make the required savings across its bilateral and multilateral programmes.

Major cuts in Belgian aid will prevent it from achieving its ODA target of 0.7% ODA/GNI

Belgium seeks, in line with its international commitments, to provide 0.7% of its gross national income (GNI) as official development assistance (ODA). This target is written into the 2013 Law on Development Cooperation (article 9). It was reconfirmed by the new government in 2014 (De Croo, 2014) and appears to be supported by Belgian taxpayers.[1] However, it is unlikely to achieve this target. Between 2010 and 2014, Belgium's net ODA and its share of GNI fell significantly – from a peak of USD 3 billion (constant USD 2012) and 0.64% of GNI to USD 2.4 billion and 0.45% of GNI (Figure 3.1). With further cuts planned between 2015 and 2019, Belgium will not be in a position to deliver on its commitment in the medium-term; indeed, ODA as a share of GNI is expected to fall to 0.38% in 2019 (FPS FA, 2015).

There is no signal from the government on when the aid budget might grow once again, or on the economic conditions that would enable Belgium to plan and set out a timeline for reaching its 0.7% target. Creating a plan could bolster the credibility of Belgium's commitments as well as the predictability of future aid allocations for its partner countries and organisations.

Figure 3.1 Belgium's net ODA: trends in volume and as a share of GNI, 1998 – 2014p

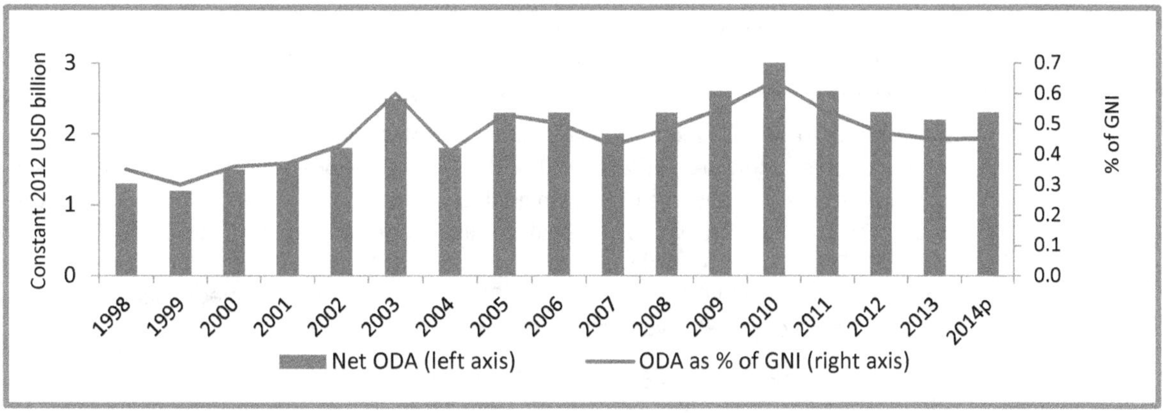

Source: DAC CRS; *Note*: p=preliminary

DGD needs to manage the budget cuts between now and 2019 strategically

While the budgetary outlook is negative,[2] clarifying the savings that need to be made by 2019 has increased the overall predictability of the budget, which will help DGD's programme planning and implementation. Compared to the multiannual forecasts for ODA in previous Federal budgets, the budget will fall by EUR 750 million over 2015 to 2019.[3]

DGD has some lead-in time to develop its strategy and criteria for applying significant cuts in 2017,[4] but it needs to do this transparently. It also needs to ensure that its approach is coherent with the government's priority of increasing the focus of its aid on fewer partner countries and multilateral organisations and of finding greater synergies with other aid channels, notably non-governmental actors. Since the criteria for applying cutbacks have not yet been identified or communicated by DGD, partners are uncertain about future support.

Forward-looking information is available through a variety of channels

On the whole, Belgium complies with the OECD recommendations on terms and conditions of aid and good pledging practice (OECD, 1978; 2011).

Belgium publishes forward-looking information on its aid through several channels, including the detailed annual budget law for development co-operation which has a four-year indicative outlook; the annual DAC Survey on Aid Allocations; and the three-to-five year Indicative Cooperation Programmes with priority countries, which contain indicative spending plans (Chapter 5). However, it will need to do more to improve the annual predictability of its bilateral disbursements in order to reach the effective aid target of 90% of funding disbursed as scheduled by 2015 (OECD/UNDP, 2014). Annual and medium-term predictability were 78% in 2013. However, Belgium's allocations to NGOs and multilateral partners are predictable over several years, which is highly appreciated by these partners.

Bilateral ODA allocations

Indicator: Aid is allocated according to the statement of intent and international commitments

Overall, Belgium's bilateral ODA allocations reflect its geographic focus on Africa and LDCs. Its sectoral priorities are less evident in aid allocations, notably the productive sectors and especially agriculture. Belgium's country programmable aid is relatively low and one quarter is channelled to non-governmental actors. Belgium still needs to deliver on its policy commitments of concentrating 50% of total ODA on LDCs and reducing fragmentation in its aid portfolio.

Allocations of total bilateral aid do not adequately reflect Belgium's geographic priorities and contribute to the dispersion of aid

In 2013, USD 1.3 billion (EUR 969 million) of Belgian ODA was provided bilaterally. This is the equivalent of 57% of total net ODA. DGD managed 74% of bilateral aid in 2013 (DGD, 2013).

Geographic allocations tend to reflect Belgium's strategic priorities. There is a strong focus on the poorest countries: in 2013, 70% of ODA was allocated to Sub-Saharan Africa, compared to the DAC average of 34%. In addition, 17 of Belgium's 18 priority countries are among the top 20 recipients of its bilateral aid (Annex B, Table 4).[5] In 2013, 0.16% of Belgium's GNI went to least developed countries as ODA, meaning that Belgium has met the UN target of giving 0.15%-0.20% of its GNI to LDCs. In order to meet its stated target of 0.25%, however, it will have to allocate even more aid to these countries.

As outlined in Chapter 2, Belgium has committed to concentrate more of its ODA on its priority countries, which will be reduced from 18 to 14; to allocate 50% of total aid to LDCs; and to increase its focus on fragile states. However, aid allocations for 2013 show that Belgium has some way to go to achieve these objectives. While the share of Belgium's bilateral aid allocable by region to LDCs was high, at 66% in 2013 (USD 405 million), total ODA to LDCs was 35.4%, lower than Belgium's 50% target (Annex B, Table 6).[6] In addition, Belgium's support to fragile states reached USD 465.4 million in 2013, accounting for 34% of total bilateral ODA. This seems low given the country's stated focus on fragile states. Nevertheless, it should be noted that in 2013, 62% of DGD's budget for governmental co-operation was allocated to fragile states. Moreover, Belgium continues to provide significant support for the Great Lakes region, in particular the Democratic Republic of the Congo, followed by Burundi and Rwanda (Figure 3.2).

Translating Belgium's policy commitments into ODA allocations and reducing the dispersion of Belgian aid are challenging tasks for several reasons:

- A small share of Belgian bilateral aid is earmarked for its 18 priority countries (24% in 2013). This share has declined from 45% in 2012-13 due to budgetary cutbacks and the reduction in debt relief operations.
- Country programmable aid as defined by the OECD is relatively low. It stood at 28% in 2013 compared to the DAC average of 54.5% (Figure 3.3).
- Different geographic criteria apply to the three main bilateral budget lines that DGD manages.[7] For example, BIO and non-governmental development actors can allocate ODA to 52 developing countries and each has a different list (although 45 countries nevertheless appear on both lists).

Figure 3.2 Belgium's bilateral ODA to its priority countries, 2013

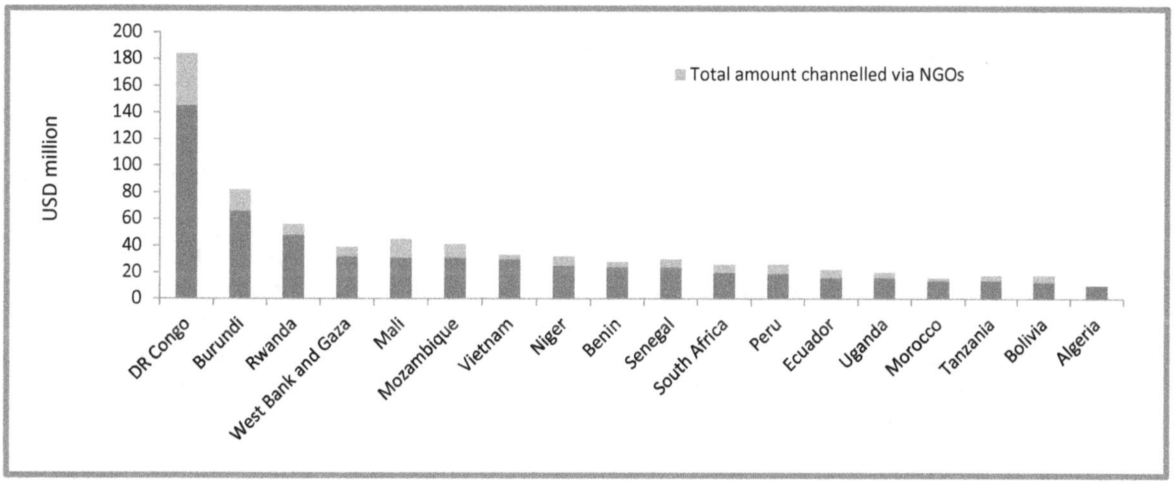

Source: DAC CRS

Figure 3.3 Composition of Belgium's bilateral ODA, 2013, gross disbursements

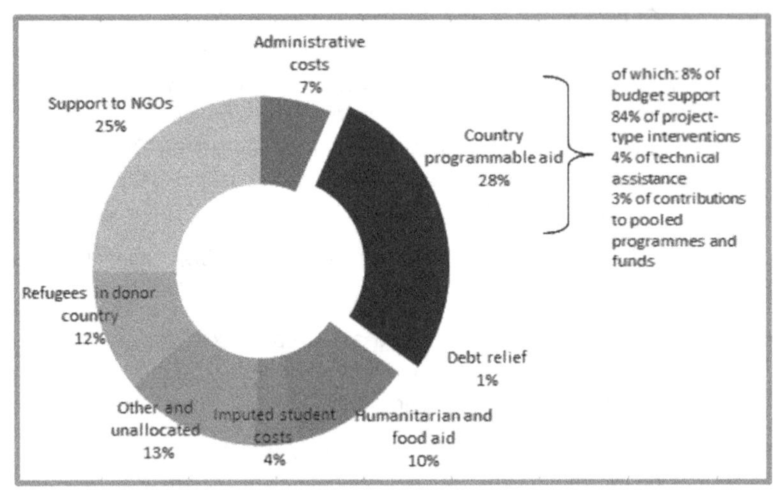

Source: DAC CRS

Bilateral aid focuses mainly on social sectors; the share of aid to productive sectors has declined

Belgium's sectoral allocations reflect its priorities.[8] In 2012-13 the largest share of bilateral sector-allocable aid went to social infrastructure and services (37%). The rest of the social sector allocations were more evenly spread: 14% to education, 9% to health and 7% to government and civil society, all of which are priorities (Annex B, Table 5).

The planned increased focus on the productive sectors, referred to in the last peer review, is however not apparent in the aid data.[9] The volume of ODA to the productive sectors has actually decreased.[10] Belgium also committed to spend 15% of total aid on agriculture by 2015. According to DGD's calculations, it is not far off this commitment, with total ODA spending on agriculture at 13.4% in 2013. However, there was only a 1% increase in the share of sector-allocable aid to agriculture, which reached 9% in 2012-13 (Annex B, Table 5).

There is a clear move in recent Indicative Cooperation Programmes (ICPs) to reduce the fragmentation of bilateral government aid within countries.[11] In reality, however, sectoral allocations to priority partner countries are spread thinly across a range of sectors and existing projects from previous ICPs. In Rwanda, there is scope to rationalise the number of projects that Belgium supports by taking a more sector-wide and programmatic approach as it does in health (Annex C).

Belgium screens a high share of its ODA against the DAC gender equality marker (Table 3.1). Despite the fact that in 2013, 71% of Belgium's total sector allocable aid helped promote gender equality, activities in which this was a principal objective represented only a small share (7.6%). Although the data do give an idea of the proportion of aid focused on this issue, especially as a principal objective, they do not allow an assessment of the extent to which gender equality and women's empowerment are integrated into the co-operation programme (Chapter 2). Efforts must be made to reinforce monitoring and evaluation systems so they can measure the impact of programmes on strengthening gender equality and women's rights.

The share of environment-focused bilateral ODA has been increasing since 2007. In 2013, 34% of Belgium's bilateral aid supported the environment, and 18% focused particularly on climate change (Figure 3.4). This was higher than the respective DAC country averages of 23% and 16%.

Table 3.1 Gender equality focus of Belgium's bilateral sector-allocable aid, 2012-13

	Constant 2012 USD million	
	2012	**2013**
Principal objective	94	64
Significant objective	303	478
Not targeted	229	218
Not screened	81	84
Total sector-allocable aid	707	844
Gender equality focused aid*	63%	71%
Memo :		
Total non-sector-allocable aid	631	502
Aid to women's equality organisations	3	3

Source: (Creditor Reporting System) CRS Aid Activity database: www.oecd.org/dac/stats/gender.

*Note:** % of sector allocable aid. Activities not screened against the gender equality marker have been excluded.

Figure 3.4 Belgium's bilateral ODA for global and local environment objectives, 2008-13

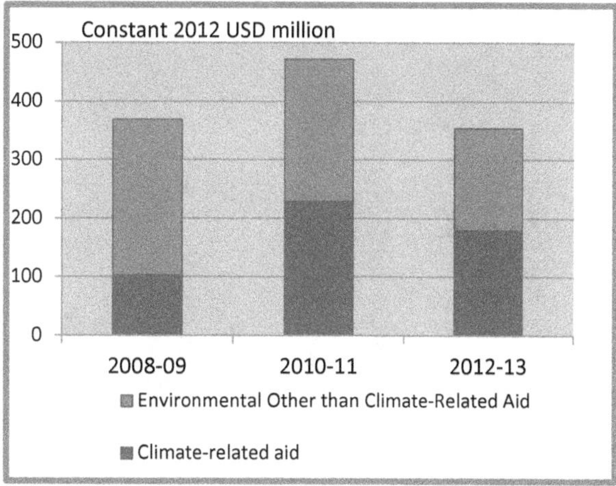

Source: (Creditor Reporting System) CRS Aid Activity database: www.oecd.org/dac/stats/gender.

Multilateral ODA channel

Indicator: The member uses the multilateral aid channels effectively

Belgium's commitment to allocate effective and predictable aid to multilateral organisations is corroborated by key partners and is reflected in its allocations. A key priority for the government is to reduce the diffusion of multilateral aid in order to strengthen the focus on strategic priorities.

Belgium is strengthening the strategic and effective use of multilateral aid

Belgium's priority for multilateral co-operation, as an essential part of its foreign and development co-operation policy, is evident in its aid allocations (Chapter 2). For example:

- It allocated, on average, 38% of total ODA to multilateral organisations between 2011 and 2013 (Annex B, Table 6).
- It provides the greatest share of its funding to multilateral organisations as core contributions (Figure 3.5).[12]
- It channelled 13% of its bilateral ODA in 2013 to specific projects implemented by multilateral organisations. 78% of these earmarked allocations went to fragile states and situations.

Figure 3.5 Belgium's support to the multilateral system, 2013, USD million

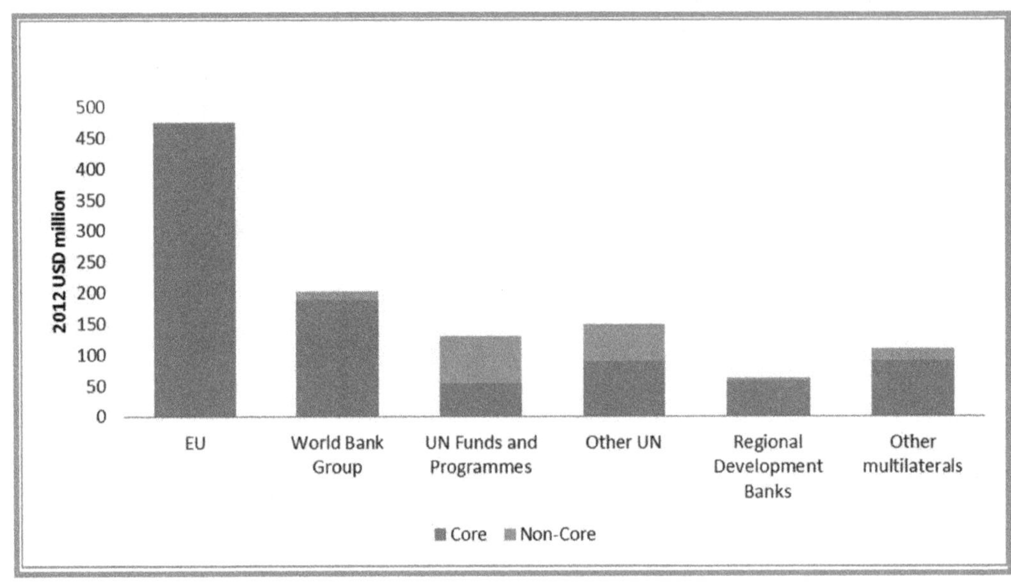

Source: DAC CRS

Belgium wants to concentrate on fewer multilateral organisations to increase efficiency and impact. Given that the 2015 budget foresees a EUR 20 million cut to DGD's multilateral budget, it needs to be even more strategic in how it allocates a declining budget.

While the 2013 Law on Development Cooperation stipulates that Belgium should contribute to a maximum of 20 multilateral partner organisations, this ceiling only applies to organisations receiving voluntary contributions. Several other (25-30) organisations above and beyond the 20 core organisations are eligible for funding. This means that Belgium's support is rather fragmented and its focus on the core priorities of the 20 multilateral partners is diluted. Belgium should therefore define clear and transparent criteria for funding and partnering with multilaterals, ensuring these criteria guide decisions, including in partner countries and fragile states.

Notes

1. According to Eurobarometer 82.1, the proportion of respondents in Belgium who say it is important to help people in developing countries is close to the EU average (84% vs. 85%), and represents a one percentage point increase since 2013 (EC, 2014).

2. These budgetary cutbacks are part of Belgium's economic and financial context of aiming to balance the national budget in 2018. All federal government departments are required to cut back on budget and administrative costs.

3. According to the government, the ODA cuts will be less than those affecting other federal government departments. This is due in part to the enshrining in law of the 0.7% target, as the government does not want to deviate too far from it. Compared with the 2014 budget, the 2015 budget contains a 10% reduction for DGD's budget, while other departments face 20% cuts. In 2019 the co-operation budget will be down by 20%, compared with 30% for the other departments. On the other hand, personnel costs must be reduced by 4% in 2015 and by 2% annually from 2016 to 2019 across the board, with no distinction made for development co-operation.

4. DGD avoided downscaling existing programmes in 2015 and 2016 by achieving the requested cuts through its contribution to the International Development Association's IDA17 Replenishment, where it opted for a nine-year encashment schedule.

5. Algeria is the only priority country that is not in the top 20 recipients.

6. In particular, an increase in the share of ODA to NGOs that is then channelled to LDCs would help the government to meet its objective of channelling 50% of total ODA to LDCs.

7. The three lines are the programme for governmental co-operation; the programme for co-operation with non-governmental actors and the programme for the private sector (BIO). (FPS Foreign Affairs, 2014: 22).

8. "DGD's strategic framework corresponds to the new law with four focus sectors: healthcare, education and training, agriculture and food security and basic infrastructure. Three thematic priorities: human rights and child rights; decent work; consolidation of society. Two cross-cutting themes: gender and climate, environment and natural resources." (DGD, 2014).

9. It was noted in the 2010 peer review that Belgium intended to increase its focus on the productive sectors by stipulating that one of the two or three priority sectors must also include a productive sector (OECD, 2010).

10. From an average of USD 171 million for the period 2007 to 2011 to USD 120 million in 2012-13.

11. For example, Bolivia's ICP focuses on health and agricultural development (water/irrigation and forestry; see http://diplomatie.belgium.be/fr/binaries/pic_bolivia_2014-2016_tcm313-158642.pdf), and Mozambique's on agriculture and renewable energy in rural areas (see http://diplomatie.belgium.be/fr/binaries/pic_mozambique_2013-2017_tcm313-158659.pdf).

12. In 2013, IFAD, ILO, UNFPA and the WHO received more non-core contributions than core, while FAO UNDP, UNICEF and WFP received more core contributions.

Bibliography

Government sources

De Croo A. (2014), "Exposé d'orientation politique – coopération au développement", Minister for Development Cooperation, Digital Agenda, Telecoms and Postal Services, Doc 54 0020/017, 14 November 2014, the Chamber of Representatives, Brussels.

DGD (2014), "Plan de management 2013-2019", unpublished document, Directorate-General for Development Cooperation and Humanitarian Aid, Brussels.

DGD (2013), *Annual Report 2012 on Belgian Development Cooperation*, FPS Foreign Affairs, Trade and Development Cooperation, Brussels.

FPS FA (2015), *Budget Général des Dépenses 2015*, FPS FA, Brussels.

FPS FA (2014), *Examen par les pairs de la Belgique 2015 - Mémorandum*, [OECD DAC Peer Review of Belgium: Memorandum], FPS FA, Brussels.

Other sources

EC (2014), "Citizens' views ahead of the European Year for Development", *Eurobarometer* 82.1, Results for Belgium, European Commission, Brussels.

OECD (2011), *DAC Recommendation on Good Pledging Practice*, OECD, Paris.

OECD (2010), *OECD Development Assistance Peer Reviews: Belgium 2010*, OECD Publishing, Paris, http://dx.doi.org/10.1787/9789264098268-en.

OECD (1978), *DAC Recommendation on Terms and Conditions of Aid*, OECD, Paris.

OECD/UNDP (2014), *Making Development Co-operation More Effective: 2014 Progress Report*, OECD Publishing, Paris, http://dx.doi.org/10.1787/9789264209305-en.

Chapter 4: Managing Belgium's development co-operation

Institutional system

Indicator: The institutional structure is conducive to consistent, quality development co-operation

Institutional reform has strengthened DGD's capacity to steer and oversee Belgian development co-operation. Nevertheless, as the context and role of development co-operation continue to evolve, DGD and other Belgian actors will need to strengthen their co-ordination in order to maximise synergies and translate them into activities in the field. Further efforts to decentralise development co-operation and to adapt BTC's business model should help Belgium improve the effectiveness of its assistance.

DGD has strengthened its strategic leadership role

Successive institutional reforms have helped strengthen the strategic leadership and direction of Belgian development co-operation in accordance with its national priorities and international commitments.

Development co-operation is the responsibility of the Directorate-General for Development Cooperation and Humanitarian Aid (DGD), which is part of the FPS Foreign Affairs (see the organisational charts in Annex D). DGD manages 60% of the development assistance budget, with the other 40% mainly allocated as European contributions and to cover internal costs (FPS Foreign Affairs, 2014a and Chapter 3). DGD, under the authority of the Minister of Development Cooperation, devises strategies, allocates funds, and monitors and assesses development co-operation programmes and projects.

A new Strategic Committee enables DGD to play a stronger leadership role – the committee agrees on policies and strategies before they are submitted to the minister for approval.[1] Strategies are then rolled out at Directorate-General level through a management plan[2] containing a series of objectives and indicators that are monitored on a six-month basis. These are translated into operational plans in each Directorate, with individual evaluation cycles.[3]

Moreover, the creation of a new Thematic Directorate, D2, brings together expertise in all the sectors and themes of Belgian development co-operation, including humanitarian aid (Chapter 7). It helps DGD to better prepare and ensure implementation of strategic guidance, in accordance with the recommendations of the previous peer review (OECD, 2010).

Management contracts signed between the government and the main co-operation actors – BTC and BIO – have made it easier to define their strategic framework.

Belgium's co-ordination mechanisms work well when they have a strategic focus

The oversight capacity of Belgian development co-operation and the role of the main actors responsible for implementing official development assistance have been reinforced. The fourth management contract between BTC and DGD clarifies the division of labour without making any fundamental changes to the terms of the previous contract. The first management contract between BIO and DGD provides a clearer framework for its role as a development actor (Chapter 1).

Belgian development co-operation is not limited to DGD, BTC and BIO, however. DGD interacts with a large number of players at the federal level – in particular the directorates-general at FPS Foreign Affairs responsible for bilateral and multilateral affairs. Relations with the other directorates at FPS Foreign Affairs are co-ordinated by the Ministry's Strategic Committee. To this end, FPS Foreign Affairs has put in place several ad hoc formal and informal consultation structures. These include monthly meetings on the Sahel and bi-monthly meetings on Central Africa, attended by FPS Foreign Affairs, FPS Interior, FPS Finance, the Defence ministry, FPS Justice (State Security) and the Coordination Unit for Threat Assessment (CUTA). These examples of whole-of-government policy and security consultation result in coherent and properly identified interventions. Some structures have been created for specific issues, such as food security (Box 4.1), development finance and the post-2015 agenda. Ad hoc interdivisional consultation helps deal with crises like the Ebola outbreak and the conflict in Syria. That said, co-ordination at headquarters is not always reflected in the field, as the review observed in Rwanda (Annex C).

The federated entities of Flanders, Wallonia-Brussels International and Brussels-Capital have their own development co-operation legislation and policy frameworks, while also having specific competence in areas likely to affect development in partner countries, such as trade. Co-ordination between the federal and federated levels is now improving following a difficult period caused by a lack of clarity over how the competence for development co-operation would evolve between the federal and federated levels respectively. Six-monthly meetings are the main mechanism for information exchange. These meetings could also be used to establish a common vision for development and better coherence and complementarity among interventions. There is no shortage of subjects to discuss, with the main issues currently being the post-2015 agenda for sustainable development, the fight against climate change, the Busan Declaration and the EU's Agenda for Change.

Box 4.1 Multi-actor discussions on food security

The Belgian Fund for Food Security is a parliamentary initiative which brings together representatives from the federal administration, BTC, NGOs and academia in a unique development programme designed to improve food security in specific regions. It helped draft the policy report on agriculture and food security, which is monitored by DGD. It can also bring in other actors depending on the issues in question. The co-ordination of Belgian positions on food security is carried out by COORMULTI.

More integrated country programmes have the potential to reinforce co-ordination but fall short of a whole-of-government approach

In the field, co-ordination among the various aid actors demonstrates the pragmatism of the Belgian approach.

The mission to Rwanda confirmed that the embassy and the local BTC representation maximise their respective roles and comparative advantages (Annex C). The fourth management contract has enabled BTC to become involved earlier in the programming process, which further strengthens co-ordination. The One Roof project, which aims to provide shared accommodation for DGD and BTC in countries where it is possible, can also help to improve co-ordination and communication. In addition to extending this clustering to all partner countries, another step in the right direction would be to set up joint representation between DGD and BTC to facilitate the implementation of the joint programme and streamline resource management.[4] However, co-ordination with BIO remains limited as it has no local representation; nevertheless recent efforts have allowed the agency to be involved in the preparation of joint commissions with partners. Finally, there have been examples of co-ordination between the federal and federated entities in partner countries, such as in Mozambique (Box 4.2).

Nonetheless, country policies are essentially limited to the activities and actors of government-to-government co-operation. In accordance with the Busan partnership principle, a more integrated approach to programming should help strengthen synergies with the activities implemented by other Belgian development co-operation actors such as NGOs. But it is not yet possible to have a whole-of-government country strategy given that Belgium does not plan to include Belgian government actors present in developing countries that are not involved directly in development co-operation.

Box 4.2 Co-operation between BTC and Flemish development co-operation in Mozambique

Since 2006, Flemish development co-operation has provided annual financing of EUR 2 million to the "Prosaude" basket fund for the health sector managed by the Government of Mozambique. Following question marks over the quality of the handling of public finances, the donors and the Ministry of Health launched an action plan covering, among other things, tighter management of these finances. In this context, in 2013 the Flemish government funded a BTC technical specialist to support the working group administering the basket fund, which helped improve financial management at the Ministry of Health.

Source: the official website of the Flemish government, http://www.flanders.be/en.

Inadequate delegation to the field is hampering institutional progress

Since the last peer review, DGD has stepped up efforts to improve co-ordination between the main Belgian development co-operation actors and reinforce their capacity to deliver effective assistance. The reform of DGD in 2012 – motivated by the need to cut red tape, reduce costs and strengthen its role – helped clarify DGD's vision, values and new missions and simplify its structure.[5] The Strategic Committee – which drives consultation and looks for opportunities for cross-cutting collaboration – and "trans-directional" teams should also enable greater coherence and co-ordination.

Further effort will be required, however, to improve communication between DGD and the embassies as staff feel that instructions are sometimes out of touch with the reality on the ground (FPS Personnel & Organisation, 2013).[6] Communication issues, coupled with the lack of financial delegation at the country level, limit the embassies' ability to fulfil their strategic role in accordance with the Busan commitments on responsible co-operation. Belgium's decentralisation efforts need to be stepped up.[7]

The fourth management contract between DGD and BTC confirmed the priority given to strengthening capacities for creating more diverse roles and responsibilities for personnel on the ground. Moreover, following a mission in the Democratic Republic of the Congo, BTC is examining ways of adapting its organisational model in the country, by strengthening the principle of subsidiarity for example (Box 4.3). This specific case could act as a model for adjusting BTC's programming structures in other fragile states. Nevertheless, despite these changes, the agency continues to operate in project mode, and inflexible procedures reduce its ability to adapt to changing contexts once projects are under way (Chapter 5).

Box 4.3 Adapting systems to the challenges of working in fragile states

A BTC mission to DRC in October 2014 looked at how to improve the efficiency and effectiveness of the programme, especially:

- streamlining the organisational model
- reinforcing quality control systems
- clarifying roles and responsibilities, specifically the functions that could be decentralised; job descriptions; specific mandates, including expanding management tasks to look at issues like quality; and modifying systems descriptions
- adapting the human resources policy to DRC's specific context.

A significant number of changes were proposed as a result of the mission, including:

- decentralising, not only from Brussels to the country office, but also from the country office to the field locations where programmes are implemented
- putting more people in the field and adapting human resources policies and incentives to the difficult working conditions
- adapting procurement systems
- simplifying the decision-making hierarchy to no more than three layers.

The report was accompanied by an outline of how the restructuring plans would be financed, and included a detailed work plan and timeframe for implementing the changes.

Source: BTC (2014d), "Rapport de la Mission Interdépartementale en RDC", unpublished document, Belgian Technical Cooperation, Brussels.

Adaptation to change

Indicator: The system is able to reform and innovate to meet evolving needs

Belgium has been investing in organisational change. To deliver on its reform, DGD will need to continue to work with staff to enable them to change working practices.

Belgium is changing its system but needs to be clear about future changes that will be required

The Belgian government is actively reorganising its institutions and trying to deal with evolving needs. For example, DGD carried out an audit so that staff could raise concerns they had with the reform and created working groups and steering groups to reinforce collaboration and information exchange. These groups included development attachés in the field (FPS Personnel & Organisation, 2013). In addition, the 2012 reform of DGD responded to both the practical need to manage the constant decline in staff numbers and the strategic requirement to strengthen the Directorate-General's role as a decision-making and knowledge centre for development co-operation (Chapter 6).

Progress in implementing the reform is monitored on a semi-annual basis under the 2013-2019 management plan (DGD, 2014b). However, DGD is running behind the initial schedule and there are delays with implementing most of the objectives, owing to political changes since 2012 and the upheaval that the reform is causing for concerned actors in terms of changes in working practices.

According to staff, a key challenge with implementing the reform at DGD is that the services and directorates are used to functioning vertically via tasks/files/countries rather than horizontally (FPS Personnel & Organisation, 2013). Despite efforts undertaken to consult and communicate about the reform, to overcome this resistance to change DDG will need to renew its efforts to get staff on board. The current climate of budget consolidation affecting personnel, the operating structure and investments, further complicates the implementation of the reform.

Rigid procedures hamper capacity to innovate

By working more closely with non-traditional development co-operation actors, in particular universities and research centres, Belgium is demonstrating its openness and its willingness to better understand how specific development issues are evolving such as the environment and fragile states. Nevertheless, this effort is not reflected in how it delivers its development co-operation given limited flexibility in programming procedures and aid modalities (Chapter 5).

Human resources

Indicator: The member manages its human resources effectively to respond to field imperatives

The succession of budget restrictions and the reforms to human resources management at FPS Foreign Affairs require it to review how it will retain development expertise in the administration and in the field. Key concerns that need to be addressed at the field level is the mobility of DGD staff to move between headquarters and the field and training opportunities for staff based in embassies.

DGD has made little progress in human resources management

The previous peer review identified human resources management, especially in DGD, as a major issue for Belgian development co-operation (OECD, 2010). Since then, little progress has been made as DGD has been hit hard by staff cuts that will continue over the coming years. These cuts are affecting both headquarters and the network of attachés working in Belgian embassies or country offices. Staff numbers at headquarters fell from 173 in 2010 to 150 in 2014 (133 officials in *'carrière interne'* careers and 17 in *'carrière externe'*). There were also 73 attachés in 2014. The fact that 61 people, including 22 attachés, will be retiring from 2019, suggests that the situation could worsen. These staff reductions are compounded by high levels of staff turnover, resulting in a loss of institutional memory and expertise.

To alleviate these difficulties, FPS Foreign Affairs has put in place various administrative solutions and measures to access and buy-in external expertise. Efforts to maintain a critical mass of development expertise within the ministry are vital, given the merger of different career lines within the Ministry of Foreign Affairs and the limited possibilities for the staff category *'carrière interne'* to work in the field. DGD needs the right expertise if it is to deliver effectively its mandate of leading the system strategically, engaging in policy dialogue and monitoring partnerships.

BTC currently employs 183 people in its headquarters, plus 253 expatriates[8] and 1 000 staff in Belgium's 18 partner countries. Even though it has had to face similar problems to DGD in terms of personnel restrictions, with 202 fewer staff since 2010, it has nevertheless managed to preserve qualified expertise in development co-operation and a strong presence in the field. Moreover, the creation of an incentive system[9] enables the agency to mobilise sufficient expertise, even in demanding situations such as fragile states. All the same, as observed in Rwanda, BTC is having problems retaining local staff with the required expertise because its salaries are not always as competitive as those paid by other donors.

Unlike the other governmental development co-operation actors, staff numbers at BIO are stable, with 40 people working at the headquarters. The staff profile is slightly more diversified now, and includes expertise in development and the environment, reflecting the agency's strategy.

There is a strong demand for training from staff in the field; BTC is actively continuing to train its personnel

Staff training at DGD is set out in an annual plan based on the needs submitted by the services, directorates and personnel, and includes both administrative topics and more technical subjects related to development co-operation. The fact that some joint training courses are carried out with personnel from BTC strengthens the common vision for development co-operation and is a pragmatic use of resources. Nevertheless, the mission to Rwanda revealed a strong demand for staff training in the field. To this end, and owing to the difficulties for the ministry's internal civil service staff to work in the field, the annual 'DGD days' play an important role in ensuring that personnel at headquarters and on the ground have a regular opportunity to meet and talk.

BTC is very active in personnel training, offering an annual average of five days training per staff member and a strong level of involvement in the Learn4Dev network. By offering coaching to its local employees and giving them the opportunity to enrol on training courses, BTC is also trying to strengthen local capacity in partner countries. Nevertheless, the funding available for training local staff is only enough for courses in the country in question, which do not always meet needs. Regional training, including courses organised by third parties, could be an option worth examining.

At BIO, training first and foremost responds to the company's needs, with annual courses on core subjects. Individual training is available based on job-related requirements.

Notes

1. The fact that the Head of the Policy Cell under the Minister of Development Cooperation is on this committee helps in making decisions on DGD's policy.

2. The latest management plan (for 2013-2019) was developed under the previous government by the Directorate-General (DGD, 2014b). Although the plan dates back to before the March 2013 Law on Development Cooperation and Humanitarian Aid, its policies are consistent with the law's objectives (Chapter 2). The management plan is linked to a series of objectives and indicators covering policy coherence, aid effectiveness and results-based management, the fight against poverty, prioritising LDCs and fragile states, and improving complementarity between humanitarian aid and development co-operation.

3. The management plan has already been used to draw up job descriptions and staff objectives for the annual performance evaluation cycle.

4. Some other DAC members have similar arrangements (e.g. Norway and Austria in some partner countries) and these have increased aid effectiveness.

5. The reform saw the structure of the Directorate-General scaled back to four Directorates, with the Directorate responsible for Multilateral and European Programmes (D4) replaced by a Thematic Directorate (D2). The other major changes involved the creation of a unit within D2 dedicated to the coherence of development-focused policies; a new service for monitoring funding allocated to NGOs in the Civil Society Directorate (D3); and the development education service, risk department and results and quality service were merged into a single Results and Quality Care department within the Organisation Management Directorate (D4), which also contains the Communication Department (Annex D).

6. In the recent report on internal communication at DGD, DGD representatives in the field indicated a lack of co-ordination and consultation between services at headquarters. There is still a high level of compartmentalisation and some instructions seem "disconnected" from the field.

7. Decentralisation is mainly visible in the programming and follow-up of ICPs, and in the quality control of projects' technical and financial files, which is now carried out jointly by the embassy and the BTC representation. In the event of a discrepancy, the file is submitted to BTC's Quality Control Committee at a meeting in Brussels attended by DGD D1, and budget support files are submitted directly to this committee.

8. Technical assistants, juniors and staff in embassies/country offices.

9. These incentives include, for example, additional leave, additional guidance and professional recognition that is useful for career development.

Bibliography

Government sources

BIO (2014), *Sustainable Human Development by Strengthening the Private Sector in Developing Countries, Annual report 2013,* Belgian Investment Company for Developing Countries, Brussels.

BTC (2014a), "General organisational structure of BTC", Belgian Technical Cooperation, Brussels.

BTC (2014b), "Plan d'action formation 2014", BTC, Brussels.

BTC (2014c), *Annual Report 2013*, BTC, Brussels.

BTC (2014d), "Rapport de la mission interdépartementale en RDC", unpublished document, Belgian Technical Cooperation, Brussels.

BTC (2014e), "Learning and Development Strategy", BTC, Brussels.

BTC (2012), "Principes de gestion des ressources humaines de la CTB", BTC, Brussels

DGD (2014a), "Organisational structure of the Directorate-General for Development Cooperation and Humanitarian Aid", Directorate-General for Development Cooperation and Humanitarian Aid, Brussels.

DGD (2014b), "Plan de management 2013-2019", unpublished document, DGD, Brussels.

DGD (2013a), *La coopération belge au développement dans les pays à revenus intermédiaires – Note stratégique*, March 2013, DGD, Brussels.

DGD (2013b), *Rapport annuel 2012 sur la Coopération belge au Développement,* FPS Foreign Affairs, Trade and Development Cooperation, Brussels.

FPS FA (2015), *Budget Général des Dépenses 2015*, FPS FA Brussels.

FPS FA (2014a), *Examen par les pairs de la Belgique 2015 - Mémorandum*, [OECD DAC Peer Review of Belgium: Memorandum], FPS FA, Brussels.

FPS FA (2014b), "Organisational structure", FPS FA, Brussels.

FPS Personnel and Organisation (2013), "Stratégie de communication interne de la DG Coopération au Développement et Aide Humanitaire. Rapport final", FPS Personnel and Organisation, Brussels.

Kingdom of Belgium (2014b), *Arrêté royal portant assentiment au quatrième contrat de gestion entre l'État belge et la société anonyme de droit public à finalité sociale "Coopération Technique Belge»*, 2 April 2014, Moniteur Belge, Brussels.

Other sources

CNCD 11.11.11 (2014), *Modernisation ou instrumentalisation de l'aide? Rapport 2014 sur l'aide belge au développement,* National Centre for Development Cooperation, Brussels.

CNCD 11.11.11 (2013), *Rapport annuel d'activités 2013,* CNCD, Brussels.

HLF4 (2011), *Busan Partnership for Effective Development Co-operation* Fourth High Level Forum on Aid Effectiveness, www.oecd.org/dac/effectiveness/49650173.pdf.

OECD (2010), *OECD Development Assistance Peer Reviews: Belgium 2010,* OECD Publishing, Paris, http://dx.doi.org/10.1787/9789264098268-en.

Chapter 5: Belgium's development co-operation delivery and partnerships

Budgeting and programming processes

Indicator: These processes support quality aid as defined in Busan

Since the last peer review, DGD has introduced a number of reforms to its country programming process in order to increase the quality of its aid. New programming guidelines aim to speed up project cycle management, and guidelines are being updated with a view to improving DGD's use of partner systems. These reforms, once carried out, have the potential to increase the quality and effectiveness of Belgium's bilateral co-operation. Their implementation will require regular monitoring and reporting of progress.

Multi-annual budgeting gives good predictability of funding to Belgium's partners

Belgium's budgeting process allows its partners to know their funding levels several years ahead. A budget envelope is attached to each Indicative Cooperation Programme (ICP), which usually covers four years.[1] However, as noted in the last peer review and observed in Rwanda, predictability is undermined by significant delays in committing the ICP budget to programmes and projects (Annex C).[2]

To deliver its bilateral aid, Belgium uses various instruments under specific budget headings in the annual Federal budget law. The multi-annual national budget forecasts for development co-operation allocate global amounts to these budget headings, providing a certain amount of predictability. The downside is that DGD has less leeway to adapt funding to changing requirements and capacities of partner countries and to evolving contexts.[3] To tackle this problem, DGD's management plan introduces the notion of a differentiated approach and commits to developing more flexible co-operation instruments to provide a more suitable response to changing circumstances and to find the right balance between predictability and flexibility (DGD, 2014).

Country programmes are aligned to national priorities but are not flexible enough

Indicative Cooperation Programmes are negotiated with partner countries and aligned to their priorities. DGD supports joint EU programming in countries and is also trying to simplify its programming process in order to speed up the delivery of its aid. To strengthen coherence among the priority sectors in the country programmes and the projects that BTC implements, there will be more upfront involvement by the agency in designing the country programme and in identifying projects, in collaboration with the partner government.[4] The new programming guidelines also flag up the possibility of conducting joint analysis with other development partners and using existing analysis: this could be given more explicit priority in order to limit duplication and to save costs.

The government's fourth management contract with BTC gives more freedom to adapt project outputs, results and activities to a changing environment. However, changes to the specific objectives, duration, and the total budget still need approval from headquarters and the *Inspecteur des finances*, which limits flexibility.[5] DGD and BTC's plans to invest in broader sector programmes could increase flexibility and help speed up the process between programme/project identification, approval and formulation – especially if it reduces the number of technical and financial files.

It is too soon to tell whether DGD's new approach to programming will improve the timeliness and relevance of Belgium's development co-operation in its priority countries. For example, while programme design has been delegated to the embassy and BTC, headquarters continues to play a strong control function – DGD and the minister will approve at least three documents[6] in the first two phases of the programming cycle, which still leaves several administrative layers.

Belgium plans to take a more flexible approach to using country systems

Belgium is seeking to make progress towards the Busan commitment on the use of country systems. New guidelines on using country systems allow for Belgium's partial use of such systems; this is an improvement on previous guidelines which offered only two possible options: use national systems in their entirety or not at all. Better analysis of the quality of national systems will also help it to identify the extent to which Belgium will use these systems. DGD has decided that it will participate in sector budget support, although in some countries sector budget support programmes have been replaced by basket funds.[7] Belgium sees basket funds as particularly useful in fragile states and for institution building as they pave the way for greater use of country systems (Box 5.1).

Belgium has a number of instruments at its disposal to deliver government-to-government aid, but mainly uses project units that are integrated in the line ministries and jointly managed by BTC and the partner government. DGD has indicated that national execution (by the partner country) must be the default option for project implementation.[8] Moving to national execution implies that BTC will need to adapt its business model in three key ways: (i) to play a stronger role in dialogue with partners; (ii) to monitor performance; and (ii) to review its approach to capacity development and technical assistance so that the partner ministry is really in the driving seat.

DGD is taking a more systematic approach to risk management despite a risk-averse domestic context

DGD is placing greater emphasis on a more systematic approach to analysing risks and using this analysis to inform planning and programming. For example, the draft new guidelines on budget support require a more detailed risk analysis covering eight risks.[9] The broad range of risks covered by this analysis could inform DGD's overall approach to risk management. In particular, it needs to take a more systematic approach to analysing and managing political risks and to develop tools for managing risks to achieving the objectives of country programmes. In this case, the risk analysis provided by BTC country representations to headquarters could be useful.

While Belgium is willing to provide aid in risky environments, this intention is counterbalanced by a domestic political context that demands the administration shows that it is avoiding both fiduciary and security risks. This pressure diverts attention from the need to balance risk with development opportunities. It can also stifle DGD and BTC's ability to develop new ways of delivering development co-operation.

Box 5.1 Lessons from Burundi in aligning basket funds with national strategies

DGD participates in basket funds in both fragile and non-fragile contexts and is considering scaling up investments in these funds, particularly in fragile states.[1] Belgium's positive experience with the *Fonds Commun Education* in Burundi provides lessons for using this system. The fund was set up in 2007-08, primarily as a tool for harmonising donors in a heavily fragmented sector, but it operated in parallel to national systems. The fund then began to use national systems and aligned with the Government of Burundi's 2012 education strategy. The key to this success was the way in which the fund was designed, with sufficient space left to adapt and experiment as the domestic situation evolved.

Source: De Maesschalck, F. et al. (2014), *Report: Basket Funds in Fragile States*, Institute of Development Policy and Management, University of Antwerp.

Note: [1]Currently Belgium makes little use of these funds, which represented 4.4% of spending between 2005 and 2012.

An increasing share of ODA is untied

Belgium's share of untied ODA (excluding administrative costs and in-donor refugee costs) was 98.1% in 2013 (up from 96.5% in 2012). The 2013 DAC average was 83.2%.

Promoting good governance through *"tranches incitatives"* needs careful review

In some partner countries, Belgium uses financial incentives called "*tranches incitatives*" to improve governance and human rights, even when these issues are not being addressed in the programmes/projects supported by Belgium through its country programme. The underlying aim of this instrument is to deepen political and strategic dialogue with partner countries with a view to the structured promotion of specific aspects of good political/technocratic governance. However, as seen in Rwanda, these incentives are difficult to apply in practice (Annex C). Part of the problem was the poor design of performance targets and indicators, and challenges with assessing progress against the conditions. Limited dialogue with the Rwandan government during the assessment process only exacerbated these problems. Despite a weak analytical basis, Belgium decided to withhold the tranche. In light of this and other experiences with the "*tranches incitatives*",[10] Belgium should review its strategy and methodology for using "positive conditionality".

Partnerships

Indicator: The member makes appropriate use of co-ordination arrangements, promotes strategic partnerships to develop synergies, and enhances mutual accountability

As a keen supporter of EU joint programming, which is enshrined in law, and by participating in and using co-ordination arrangements, Belgium is taking forward its commitments to deliver quality development co-operation. It now needs to reinforce synergies among partners. The objectives of the reform of funding for non-governmental actors are relevant. Nevertheless, the impact of Belgian aid channelled through non-governmental actors could be increased if it were guided by a clear strategy that has civil society backing, and transparent criteria for assessing performance.

Belgium promotes joint working but needs greater capacity in embassies

Belgium adheres to the principles for making aid effective, notably through the implementation of the EU's Agenda for Change involving delegated co-operation[11] and joint programmes. This was confirmed in Rwanda, where Belgium respects and encourages the strong leadership of the government, and co-chairs two ambitious sector working groups which are high priorities for the authorities (Annex C). However, Belgium faces some challenges in delivering on its commitments and ambitions. For example, there was insufficient capacity at its very dynamic and productive embassy in Rwanda to fulfil adequately its partnership and harmonisation ambitions. It did, however, receive valuable backstopping from BTC.

Belgium engages actively in mutual accountability processes

Belgium promotes mutual accountability by negotiating and co-signing its country programmes with its priority partner countries. Progress is reviewed by Joint Commissions comprising representatives of the two governments, and committees of partners. It is clear from the mission to Rwanda that Belgium takes these reviews seriously and that they provide space for the two governments to talk about successes and challenges. In light of its good performance in this area, Belgium could increase transparency by publicising the results of the reviews, with the agreement of its partner, and could consider opening these reviews to other participants. These measures would be in line with the Busan indicator on mutual accountability (OECD/UNDP, 2014).

More integrated country programming could unite Belgium and its partners around a shared focus

Belgium delivers its support to its priority countries through a range of systems and partners. There is scope, as mentioned in the last peer review, "to take a broader and more strategic approach to engaging with partners, which could raise the visibility of Belgium's support" (OECD, 2010). In line with these suggestions, Belgium is in the process of developing a more "integrated programme", which could significantly change its way of working with partners in priority countries (FPS FA, 2014; Chapter 2). Belgian NGOs and other civil society actors met by the peer review team seem to support this initiative, which has the potential to unite all the Belgian co-operation actors – governmental and non-governmental — around common objectives, especially if it focuses on the added value of partners and strengthens the synergies between interventions.

DGD is currently clarifying the approach to integrated programming with Belgian civil society. This consultation should help it obtain buy-in, especially by Belgian non-governmental actors, which receive their funding from headquarters and fear that such an approach would undermine their right of initiative. Several DAC members (such as Australia, Denmark, Ireland, and Switzerland) have comprehensive country strategies covering a range of objectives and partners, including domestic NGOs, which could serve as examples for Belgium.

The planned common analysis of the context in priority countries by all the Belgian non-governmental actors could help identify synergies and complementarities for putting in place an integrated programme of this type. However, in order to be successful, the analysis would also need to be extended to other partners or actors delivering Belgian ODA in the priority country. Going forward, it would make sense to link this analysis to the development of country strategies.

The funding reform for non-governmental development co-operation actors needs to be guided by a clear civil society policy

A wealth of Belgian NGOs and other non-governmental actors – including universities, towns, communes, mutual insurance funds, scientific and community institutions, and trade unions – are very active in development. They attract high numbers of volunteers who are engaged in building public awareness and political campaigning for development.[12] These non-governmental actors are also major partners for delivering Belgian ODA: 24% of bilateral ODA (USD 322 million) was provided to or through these non-governmental actors in 2013 (Annex B, Table 2). Strategic and technical co-ordination committees at headquarters facilitate dialogue with these non-governmental actors.

The 2014 Royal Decree introduced a major reform to funding procedures, based on consultation with non-governmental actors, that will come into force in 2017 (Kingdom of Belgium, 2014a). The objectives of the reform – reducing fragmentation and administrative procedures and promoting a stronger results focus – are pertinent and timely.[13] The government also intends to reduce the very high transaction costs involved in managing the non-governmental actor portfolio[14] and to increase the impact of its development assistance by engaging in fewer NGO partnerships.

However, DGD is finding it difficult to implement these reforms as it has to both manage the current NGA portfolio and lay the foundations for the reforms in time for 2017. As for the NGAs, they are critical of certain aspects of the reform.[15] To temper this criticism, DGD should communicate its implementation strategy and the criteria, including performance-based criteria, which will be applied in the new accreditation process and for granting funds as of 2017.

Moreover, DGD does not have a clear policy which sets out the objectives, rationale, added value and approach to partnering with civil society (other than the statement in the 2013 Law on Development Cooperation that building civil society and support for decentralisation are objectives for co-operation with NGOs).[16] This is a major gap which needs to be filled, especially in light of the ongoing reform of civil society funding and the need to identify where to apply the planned cutbacks in funding for non-governmental actors from 2017. A formal and transparent policy for civil society could guide funding decisions approved by recent legislation.[17]

Fragile states

Indicator: Delivery modalities and partnerships help deliver quality

Belgium is an active advocate for donors to remain engaged in fragile contexts. It has flexible tools for working in these complex environments, which includes the possibility to use country systems. The moves towards greater whole-of-government coherence in fragile contexts, however, has not yet led to a common Belgian position towards its fragile partners, nor clear roles and responsibilities across government. This missed opportunity to bring Belgium's foreign policy tools together undermines efforts towards a more effective response. In addition, Belgium will need to ensure it has the right resources and delegation of authority in the field to adapt programmes to evolving situations; this may be difficult in the current context of staffing cuts.

The lack of a cross-government approach to fragile states is a missed opportunity

The 2010 peer review recommended that Belgium develop whole-of-government strategies for fragile states (OECD, 2010); this has not been done, although there have been some moves towards greater coherence. A cross-directorate team has been put together to discuss Belgium's response to Mali and Niger, for example, bringing together desk officers, fragility staff and academics. Another team for the Great Lakes region comprises diplomatic, defence and development co-operation personnel (Chapter 4). DGD is also looking to better understand the contextual risks in fragile states, and to use these to target its programming. However, there is not yet a common Belgian position towards its individual fragile state partners, nor a set of results that is shared by the different actors across government, with clearly laid out roles and responsibilities. This seems to be a missed opportunity to bring all Belgium's foreign policy tools together to support a more effective response to fragile situations.

Belgium is a keen advocate for other donors to engage in fragile contexts

Belgium is active on the international stage, advocating for other donors to remain engaged in fragile situations. It will also engage in areas where other donors are not present, such as remote areas of the Democratic Republic of the Congo. Basket funds are used to support co-ordination, for example for education in Burundi (Box 5.1).

Belgium supports statebuilding through a flexible approach, but could strengthen staff competencies in the field

In Burundi, Belgium is taking the lead on statebuilding by using country procurement systems, believing that the cost of delays in project implementation is outweighed by the gains in strengthening partner capacity. These types of programmes are based on detailed systems analyses, one of which is currently underway in Mali. In rapidly evolving situations, such as in Mali following the 2012 *coup d'état*, Belgium allocated its reserve budget to interventions by multilateral partners, although these types of changes need to be approved in Brussels[18] and must therefore abide by the risk tolerance of the *Inspecteur des finances*. As Belgium scales up its involvement in fragile states, it will need to ensure that it has the right resources in the field, including sufficient delegated authority, to ensure that programmes can be effective in these rapidly evolving environments.

Notes

1. The 2015 Budget Law (p. 19) states that DGD can make new multi-year commitments with partner countries up to a ceiling of EUR 250 million. The total size of ongoing activities must not exceed EUR 750 million.

2. Commitments are made on the basis of projects which take at least 2 years - and up to 5 years – to be approved after the ICP has been signed by both governments. Approval is only possible after identification and drafting of the Technical and Financial Dossier. According to DGD, delays in execution are caused by a lengthy project identification process. These delays apply only to government-to-government co-operation which is managed by BTC and is usually delivered through a co-managed project embedded in line ministries.

3. For example, the budget for "Country Programmes" contains eight budget headings with an indicative budget fixed until 2019 (FPS Foreign Affairs, 2015).

4. There will be an 18-month lead-in prepare the ICP.

5. The budget will still be tied to projects with very detailed technical files which are approved by the *Inspecteur des Finances*, who reviews the project files from the perspective of the legal framework and fiduciary criteria, DGD strategies, BTC and DGD risk analysis.

6. According to the instructions for the "Management Cycle for a Cooperation Programme", these are (i) the proposal for terms of reference related to BTC's contribution to the preparatory phase; (ii) the basic assessment and the draft performance monitoring matrix; and (iii) the final Co-operation Programme. The specific agreement should also be seen or approved by the minister.

7. Currently Belgium uses sector budget support in Bolivia, Burundi, West Bank and Gaza Strip, Peru and Rwanda, and new programmes are being prepared in Bolivia, Tanzania, and possibly Uganda.

8. This is in line with the commitment in the 2013 Law on Belgian Development Cooperation, which states that government co-operation favours national execution of its interventions using the procedures, instruments and management systems of the partner countries, and shall reinforce them when necessary.

9. The eight risks to be analysed are: political context, macro-economic situation, sector policy, sector dialogue, M&E system, effectiveness of the civil service, fiduciary risk, corruption.

10. This "*tranche incitative*" is also being used in Uganda linked with sector-based support to education, and in Burundi.

11. Our review of the ICPs found that while there are several examples of delegated co-operation, they are not necessarily in its priority sectors. According to DGD, this is a political choice as delegated co-operation is a means of intervening outside of priority sectors as all interventions in priority sectors are carried out by BTC. In Uganda for example, there is delegated co-operation with Denmark in the agro-industry, which is not a priority sector.

12. For example, the Flemish NGO platform 11.11.11. reports that there are 20 000 volunteers in its member organisations.

13. The conclusion of the Meta-Evaluation of Non-Governmental Development Aid Programmes (SES, 2013) was that it was impossible to assess the extent to which DGD's non-governmental co-operation as a whole effectively contributed to development.

14. DGD manages multi-annual programmes and projects with 110 NGOs. DAC's creditor reporting system had 1 001 entries for Belgium's national NGOs in 2013, with an average amount of USD 177 000.

15. There is a perception among non-governmental actors that the 2014 Royal Decree does not recognise the differences between the various types of actors. They would prefer a partnership approach to funding that focuses on the role and added value of partners and the results to be achieved. There also seems to be resistance to change. Belgian CSOs have enjoyed long-standing and significant autonomy in the focus and

nature of the programmes and projects they submit to DGD and fear that this will be lost. Moreover, many organisations, especially smaller ones, appear to be dependent on ODA.

16. In 2009, the DGDC-NGO Coordination Group approved two notes on the different roles of Belgian NGOs, their specialisations, complementarities and synergies. However, these notes do not constitute a Belgian partnership policy or strategy with civil society for development co-operation.

17. I.e. the 2014 law amending the 2013 Law on Development Cooperation and the 2014 Royal Decree governing the funding of non-governmental co-operation actors.

18. Any changes to objectives, expected results and programme timeframes have to be approved by both parties via an exchange of letters. In Belgium, the use of an exchange of letters as a specific convention is approved by the minister.

Bibliography

Government sources

BTC (2014), "Rapport de la mission interdépartementale en RDC", unpublished document, Belgian Technical Cooperation, Brussels.

DGD (2014), "Plan de management 2013-2019", unpublished document, Directorate-General for Development Cooperation and Humanitarian Aid, Brussels.

DGD (n.d), "Cycle de gestion d'un programme de coopération", unpublished document, DGD, Brussels.

DGD (n.d), "Cooperation programme aid modalities and implementation modalities", unpublished document, DGD, Brussels.

DGD (2015), *Draft Vademecum Begrotingshul* [Budget support], unpublished document, DGD, Brussels.

DGD (2012), "Note politique sur la tranche incitative", DGD, Brussels.

DGCD-ONG (2009a), "Spécialisation, complémentarité et synergies : note de consensus", unpublished document, DGCD-ONG.

DGCD-ONG (2009b), "Les différents rôles des ONG Nord : note de consensus", unpublished document, DGCD-ONG.

FPS FA (2015), *Budget Général des Dépenses 2015*, FPS Foreign Affairs, Foreign Trade and Development Cooperation, Brussels.

FPS FA (2014), *Examen par les pairs de la Belgique 2015 - Mémorandum*, [OECD DAC Peer Review of Belgium: Memorandum], FPS FA, Brussels.

Kingdom of Belgium (2014a), *Arrêté royal concernant la subvention des acteurs de la coopération non gouvernmentale*, Moniteur Belge, Brussels.

Kingdom of Belgium (2014a*), Loi modifiant la loi du 19 mars 2013 relative à la Coopération au Développement*, 9 January 2014, Moniteur Belge, Brussels.

SES (2013), *La Méta-évaluation des programmes des acteurs non-gouvernementaux,* Service de l'Évaluation spéciale de la Coopération belge au développement, Kingdom of Belgium, Brussels.

Other sources

Belgian NGOs (2015), Written submission to the peer review of Belgium, unpublished document.

OECD (2010), *OECD Development Assistance Peer Reviews: Belgium 2010,* OECD Publishing, Paris, http://dx.doi.org/10.1787/9789264098268-en.

OECD/UNDP (2014), *Making Development Co-operation More Effective: 2014 Progress Report*, OECD Publishing, Paris, http://dx.doi.org/10.1787/9789264209305-en

Chapter 6: Results-based management, learning and accountability in the Belgian programme

Policies, strategies, plans, follow-up and notification

Indicator: A results-based management system has been implemented to evaluate performance in line with partner countries' priorities, development objectives and systems

Belgium is in the process of strengthening its results culture and developing a more comprehensive follow-up and management system beyond BTC's project results measurement. Belgium wants to make results management the responsibility of its implementing partners; however, the mechanisms for consolidating the results information have yet to be clearly defined which could undermine the objective of country-level results management. Consolidating monitoring and evaluation mechanisms will be important in overcoming this challenge. In this context, Belgium should not lose sight of its current approach to using partner countries' monitoring systems to the maximum extent possible.

Belgium is investing in improving its system for managing for results, which is currently limited to projects

Following the 2010 peer review recommendation (Annex A), Belgium has been developing its approach to results-based management. The importance of this issue has been validated at the highest level and is cited in the 2013 Law on Development Cooperation.[1] In line with this, Belgium will track the results being achieved by its co-operation partners,[2] policy evaluations will pay greater attention to the measurement of results,[3] and a results department has been created at DGD.

In addition to the legal and policy framework, Belgium is striving to promote a results culture. By carrying out joint staff training in DGD and BTC, and launching a consultative process for drafting the results policy, it has fostered a shared understanding of the ideas and approach to be adopted. The results agenda has not yet been internalised, however, and there seems to be weak demand for results among the public and parliamentarians, with greatest attention being given to spending. Extra effort will be needed to strengthen this culture and translate managing for results into a daily reality for Belgian co-operation officials.

The "development results" policy, which was recently signed off by the Minister, states that a results approach should be rolled out at programme and country level, partly by drawing up a results matrix for Indicative Cooperation Programmes (DGD, 2015). At present, key concepts for managing for results are not applied universally or consistently. They are only applied at the project level.[4] Mechanisms for consolidating results frameworks are needed, otherwise Belgium runs the risk of developing a fragmented approach that will not allow it to gather the information it needs to support policy decisions.

It is currently hard to use information generated by DGD's tracking and evaluation mechanisms due to the lack of consolidated information and clear guidance for processing reports provided by partners. This can give rise to important differences in decisions taken on the basis of results. The mission to Rwanda confirmed that staff in the field do not always have a clear view of how information they provide is used. This, coupled with the fact that Belgium's sector strategies are not particularly oriented towards results, weakens DGD's ability to steer Belgian co-operation. It still needs to give clear a signal about the use of results. Extending results-based management from intervention level to sector and country level will require a more pervasive results culture.

Results measurement actively involves the partner country but is limited to projects and is rarely used to increase transparency

BTC's system for measuring project results is put together with the stakeholders and, wherever possible, uses the partner country's indicators and information systems, as confirmed during the Rwanda field visit. Information generated by the results matrix is discussed by the projects' steering committee every year and provides useful input to project management. A final monitoring report and internal evaluations are then used for communication between the field, BTC headquarters and DGD. The officials responsible for monitoring highlight the difficulty, in practice, of measuring results beyond physical outputs – a problem accentuated by the trend in Belgian co-operation towards activities focused on behaviour change rather than the provision of goods and services.

Belgian co-operation is also struggling to measure and report the results of its co-operation at a more consolidated level, as illustrated by the weak results focus of country monitoring reports. Evaluations are either done for projects[5] or at a very strategic level,[6] and cannot support decision making at programme or country level. In addition, the monitoring system does not yet inform evaluation needs. The problem could doubtless be solved by reforming the evaluation function within BTC and introducing a country-level results matrix, provided that the evaluations and completed matrix are then used.

There is no specific results approach for fragile contexts

Belgium has no specific approach to measuring results in fragile environments and the development results policy does not plan for a specific approach.

Evaluation system

Indicator: The system complies with DAC evaluation principles

Belgium's evaluation system complies with DAC principles and guarantees the independence of evaluations. Current efforts to increase the evaluation capacity of Belgian co-operation should lead to greater coverage of the portfolio, although the planned reforms may not be sufficient to ensure that evaluations are carried out at a strategic enough level. Belgium should also continue to pursue its efforts to build the evaluation capacity of partner countries, including through evaluations carried out by its partners.

Belgium has a results-focused evaluation policy

The 2013 law on development co-operation draws a distinction between external and internal evaluation, with the latter now under the responsibility of partners implementing governmental and non-governmental co-operation. Since May 2014, external evaluations have been carried out in line with the evaluation policy of the Special Evaluation Service (SES), which is aligned with the DAC's principles and quality standards, and is clearly designed to encourage the measurement of development results and the impact of Belgian co-operation. The policy also clarifies the roles and responsibilities of the Special Evaluation Service, which is now the sole body in charge of evaluation within FPS Foreign Affairs.[7]

The Special Evaluation Service is responsible for carrying out both strategic and policy evaluations, and standardising and certifying the evaluation departments of implementing partners in charge of internal evaluations. The SES has its own budget line, outside the

DGD budget, to ensure that it has the financial resources it needs to carry out these evaluations. While the SES budget seems sufficient to carry out complex, high-quality evaluations, uncertainty surrounding its staffing, combined with its new certification role, could restrict its capacity to fulfil its new mandate.

Implementing partners are in charge of their own internal evaluations. BIO and BTC are expanding their evaluation capacity but have yet to finalise their strategies in this area.

Belgium prioritises independent evaluations

Responsibility for ensuring the independence of evaluations falls largely to the SES, which is separated from the processes of policy formulation and implementation. It may consult DGD and the various partners when planning evaluations, but because it has its own budget, it is completely free to select, carry out and disseminate its evaluations. Calling on independent external evaluators should further increase the independence and impartiality of its evaluations, which are themselves evaluated during partners' certification process. For example, BTC's new evaluation department will report directly to the Managing Board. The department's independence would seem to be secure, but it must be provided with sufficient resources to fulfil its function.

There is scope to conduct sector and country-level evaluations

While mechanisms are in place for strategic and project evaluations, evaluations at the sector and country level are lacking.

BTC's interventions are subject to systematic internal evaluations. Strategic and policy evaluations are set out in a five-year programme, updated every year. A full cycle should cover a significant part of ODA and the range of partners, sectors and aid distribution channels. In practice, however, the last cycle of evaluations mostly covered aid distribution channels. Since these evaluations are designed for political decision makers and senior management, they do not examine pertinent questions at the country level,[8] where management for results really takes place.

The mandate of DGD's new results department should help ensure better alignment between evaluation programming and the needs of DGD. Moreover, the planned creation of an evaluation department at BTC should help fill the gap in country and sector evaluations, although clarification of the department's financing and evaluation programming is needed to ensure strategic coverage of the portfolio and provision of the right resources.

Belgium conducts joint evaluations but could involve partner countries better

Part of the SES's mandate is to increase the evaluation capacity of partner countries. In practice, this means involving them in evaluation exercises, usually within the wider framework of reporting exercises and joint evaluations. SES is actively engaged in carrying out joint evaluations with other donors and, to a lesser extent, with recipient countries.

Very strict rules governing BTC's internal reviews, however, give partner countries little involvement in determining the terms of reference. It must be pointed out, however, that conclusions and recommendations are discussed with partners through project steering committees. Greater strategic involvement of partner countries in evaluations will therefore need to be considered in future certification processes, allowing Belgium to increase mutual responsibility and local capacity.

Institutional learning

Indicator: Evaluations and the right knowledge management systems are used as management tools

There is scope to step up efforts to capitalise in a strategic and systematic way on the information, knowledge and expertise embodied in Belgian development co-operation. DGD and BTC are working on institutional learning, but to transform their institutions so that they better value and share knowledge they need a strategy, support from senior management and to address the challenge of getting people to use the systems for knowledge sharing.

DGD underuses evaluation findings for learning and overall programme management

DGD's success at using and learning from evaluations is mixed – despite the recommendation in the 2010 peer review. For example, the Special Evaluation Service systematically disseminates the results and lessons of the evaluations it commissions, and management responses are mandatory for all its evaluations. Yet the peer review team has heard that there is resistance to management responses in DGD: it takes longer than the agreed two months to deliver a response, which tends to be vague and lacking a timeline for action.[9] Finally, the Special Evaluator does not systematically follow up on management responses. There is scope, therefore, to review the use of evaluation feedback mechanisms so that they serve their purpose.

According to the Memorandum, "the evaluation reports sent to DGD from the different parties are automatically discussed by the managing departments" (FPS, FA, 2014). BTC and the project steering committees also discuss the recommendations made by external and internal reviews of interventions, but the evaluations and reviews are not circulated beyond these circles. This is a missed opportunity given their value as a source of lessons and good practice.

To become a knowledge centre, DGD needs a clear strategy for managing knowledge and learning from experience

One of the seven objectives in DGD's management plan is to become a knowledge centre in order to take decisions that are more evidence-based and to make projects and programmes more effective (DGD, 2014). The need to create an institutional culture that values and shares knowledge is particularly urgent: staff numbers are decreasing and fewer staff have field experience. Existing knowledge is precious (Chapter 4). An audit of DGD's internal communication recommended that it needs to "improve the management and dissemination of knowledge within DGD" (FPS Personnel and Organisation, 2013). While it does generate and share knowledge through formal and informal activities[10] and has the technology for storing information and knowledge products, it is hard to get people to use them beyond exchanging information. A strategic approach to knowledge management involving the systematic application of lessons learned would provide DGD with useful management and decision making tools.

Communication, accountability and development awareness

Indicator: The member communicates development results transparently and honestly

DGD and BTC work strategically and closely with Belgian non-governmental actors to build public awareness of development issues and support for development co-operation. DAC members can learn from this good practice. At the same time, Belgium is not on track to meet its transparency commitments. DGD needs to secure adequate capacity to maintain, update and use its new aid database to ensure greater accountability for results.

Implementing a strong commitment to transparency and accountability is proving challenging

DGD is carrying out several initiatives to increase transparency and publish timely, comprehensive and forward-looking information in line with its Busan commitments. For example, in 2011 it launched the government's open data portal and set out a timeline for publishing to the International Aid Transparency Initiative standard by 2014. However, Belgium has some way to go in achieving its transparency objectives as agreed in the Busan Partnership for Effective Development co-operation and risks missing the December 2015 deadline. Belgium rated as "very poor" in the 2014 Aid Transparency Index.[11] It has since published its first data in IATI format, however, and it plans to publish more.

DGD's online database does not contain up-to-date information about programmes, projects or ODA spending – problems it is currently addressing. And although DGD has invested resources in designing a new database, it has just one member of staff to manage all matters related to statistics and reporting. A key challenge for DGD now will be to ensure it can maintain a high-quality database over the long term, that it has the capacity to analyse the data, and that it uses results information for programme management and accountability to parliament and taxpayers.

DGD and BTC could improve communication on the results and risks of development co-operation

Communicating Belgium's contribution to development results is a priority for DGD, which has solid, evidence-based strategies for communication and development education, backed up by a relatively high budget. Yet its communication on results and risks remains weak. For example, the annual reports produced for Parliament and the public are the main channel for communicating results, but are largely based on reports by development attachés and project managers. They make only passing reference to evaluations, problems and challenges, and to the results recorded by non-governmental organisations and multilateral organisations (FPS FA, 2014: 39).

BTC's communication team has been working closely with the monitoring and evaluation team and staff based in partner countries to gather results information that can be communicated strategically to the public. Nevertheless, BTC recognises that it could also improve how it communicates its results.

DGD's approach to raising public awareness is good practice

Belgium's approach to raising public awareness of development issues (enshrined in Article 7 of the 2013 Law on Development Cooperation) shows several strengths and good practice. For example:

- The development education and communication strategies are separate but both aim to strengthen public support. Regular co-ordination between DGD's Communication and Development Education Units and the Ministry of Foreign Affairs' Central Unit for Communication builds synergies.

- DGD took a consultative approach to preparing its development education strategy (DGD, 2012); this was a key strength given that civil society organisations, BTC, schools and the regions of Flanders and Wallonia are central to implementing it.
- DGD is collaborating with NGOs to develop criteria and indicators for measuring the impact of development education (Box 6.1). Being able to show results helps justify the ODA invested in raising public awareness. In 2014, the total annual budget for communication and development education was EUR 30 million.[12]

Box 6.1 Belgian public-awareness strategies are evidence-based

In line with the DAC's lessons for engaging with the public (OECD, 2014), Belgium focuses on gathering evidence of what works and why in its development communication and education work. For example, DGD supported a multi-disciplinary study on public support for and attitudes towards development co-operation (PULSE, 2012). The research findings fed into the ministry's new communication and development education strategies. Awareness-raising projects and activities were mapped by target groups, comparing the supply of and the demand for information. In 2012, an in-depth study measuring the effects of development education programmes was financed by DGD in the framework of the research platform on public support (PULSE)

The 2013 mid-term evaluation of the *Annoncer la Couleur* programme[1] assessed its implementation and progress, and drew conclusions with a focus on education (Peeters et al., 2013). Changes were made in response to its recommendations.

Source: OECD (2014), *Engaging With the Public: Twelve lessons from DAC Peer Reviews*, OECD Publishing, Paris; Peeters, B. et al. (2013), *Évaluation à mi-parcours, Annoncer la couleur*, Kleur Bekennen, South Research CVBA-VSO, Kessel.

Notes: [1] For details see www.annoncerlacouleur.be/.

Notes

1. This law requires that the results of Belgian co-operation be evaluated and a consistent approach be taken to report the results and adopt results-based management. The DGD management plan restates the administration's intention to focus on results obtained in the field "with a view to exposing the link between the resources put in and the results achieved" and has defined results-based management as one of its seven goals for 2013-19 (DGD, 2014).

2. The latest management contract between DGD and its operatives includes the obligation to track and evaluate results. The fourth management contract between the government and BTC introduced a "best endeavours" clause for achieving the intervention's specific goals over and above a performance requirement concerning outcomes (delivery of goods and services).

3. The Belgian Development Cooperation Special Evaluation Service points out that evaluations are geared towards results analysis.

4. At project level, the baseline information and the results matrices drawn up for each intervention serve as the basis for dialogue with the partner, in order to formulate quantifiable objectives, track results and support decision making. The use of the reference situation in connection with a results matrix was developed by BTC in 2012 and implemented in 2013.

5. In this case they are carried out by co-operation operatives and are termed internal evaluations, or internal BTC reviews.

6. These evaluations refer to the exercises carried out by the Special Evaluation Service: i.e. external evaluations.

7. After the last peer review, the Special Evaluation Service merged with the DGD's evaluation units.

8. With the exception of a very few country evaluations carried out jointly with other donors.

9. A study conducted by the *Groupe de Recherche en Appui à la Politique par la DGD et la CUD* (GRAP, 2013) came up with similar findings: "a majority of management responses remain relatively vague and not very operational".

10. For example, by pooling resources in cross-directorate teams which include outside experts and people from the field in specific partner countries, such as Mali and Niger.

11. More details on the rating are available at: http://ati.publishwhatyoufund.org/donor/belgium/

12. The budget is broken down as follows: EUR 21 million for development education by NGOs, EUR 3 million for corporate communication and EUR 3 million for the *Annoncer la Couleur* programme.

Bibliography

Government sources

BIO (2014), "Outline of a development results framework for BIO", unpublished document, Belgian Investment Company for Developing Countries, Brussels.

BTC (n.d.), "Guide d'utilisation du tableau de bord monitoring opérationnel", unpublished document, Belgian Technical Cooperation, Brussels.

BTC (2015a), "Fiches descriptives des indicateurs clés de performance repris dans le plan d'entreprise 2015", unpublished document, BTC, Brussels.

BTC (2015b), "Plan d'action pays 2015 Rwanda", unpublished document, BTC, Brussels.

BTC (2015c), "Plan d'entreprise 2015", unpublished document, BTC, Brussels.

BTC (2014), "Learning and development strategy", unpublished document, BTC, Brussels.

BTC (2013a), "'More results', Directives Générales en matière de monitoring et de revue des résultats, Part I, II et III", unpublished document, BTC, Brussels.

BTC (2013b), "Rapport d'appréciation Bolivie, Programme Indicatif de Coopération 2008-2011", unpublished document, BTC, Brussels.

BTC (2012), "Note d'appréciation du programme de coopération bilatérale entre la Belgique et le Bénin, document interne préparatoire à la Commission Mixte de Novembre 2012", unpublished document, BTC, Brussels.

DGD (2015), "Résultats de développement – Note stratégique", unpublished document, Directorate-General for Development Cooperation and Humanitarian Aid, Brussels.

DGD (2014), "Plan de management 2013-2019", unpublished document, DGD, Brussels.

DGD (2013), "Communication - Note de stratégie", DGD, Brussels.

DGD (2012), "Éducation au développement - Note de stratégie", DGD, Brussels.

FPS FA (2014), *Examen par les pairs de la Belgique 2015 - Mémorandum*, [OECD DAC Peer Review of Belgium: Memorandum], Federal Public Service, Foreign Affairs, Foreign Trade and Development Cooperation, Brussels.

FPS Personnel and Organisation (2013), *Stratégie de communication interne de la DG Coopération au Développement et Aide Humanitaire, Rapport final*, SPF PO, Brussels.

Kingdom of Belgium (2014a), *Arrêté royal portant assentiment au 1er contrat de gestion entre l'État belge et la société anonyme de droit public "Société belge d'investissement pour les pays en développement"*, 2 April 2014, Moniteur Belge, Brussels.

Kingdom of Belgium (2014b), *Arrêté royal portant assentiment au quatrième contrat de gestion entre l'État belge et la société anonyme de droit public à finalité sociale "Coopération Technique Belge"*, 2 April 2014, Moniteur Belge, Brussels.

Kingdom of Belgium (2013), *Loi relative à la Coopération au Développement*, 19 March 2013, Moniteur Belge, Brussels.

SES (2014a), *Évaluation de terrain des investissements de la Société belge d'investissement pour les pays en développement (BIO)*, Special Evaluation Office for Belgian Develpment Cooperation, FPS Foreign Affairs, Foreign Trade and Development Cooperation, Brussels. http://www.bio-invest.be/fr/news/135-levaluation-sur-le-terrain-des-investissements-de-bio-confirme-leur-pertinence-et-additionalite.html.

SES (2014b), *Rapport de l'Évaluateur Spécial de la Coopération belge au développement. Rapport sur les exercices 2012 et 2013*, SES, FPS FA, Brussels, http://diplomatie.belgium.be/fr/binaries/Rapport_SES_2012-13_tcm313-263695.pdf.

SES (2014c), *"Tirer des Enseignements de l'expérience passée et rendre compte des résultats", Politique d'Évaluation, Service de l'Évaluation Spéciale de la Coopération Belge au Développement*, SES, FPS FA, Brussels.

SES (2013), *Évaluer l'impact, la quête du Graal ? Évaluation ex post de l'impact de quatre projets de coopération gouvernementale – Rapport de synthèse*, SES, FPS FA, Brussels.

SES (2012a), *Évaluation du rapportage des résultats de la Direction Générale de la Coopération au Développement (DGD)*, SES, FPS FA, Brussels.

SES (2012b), *Coming to Terms with Reality, Evaluation of the Belgian Debt Relief Policy (2000-2009)*, SES, FPS FA, Brussels.

Other sources

Aid Transparency Index (2014), Publish What You Fund, http://ati.publishwhatyoufund.org.

EC (2014), "Citizens' views ahead of the European Year for Development", *Eurobarometer* 82.1, Results for Belgium, European Commission, Brussels.

GRAP (2013), "La pratique évaluative dans la coopération belge : constats et perspectives", *Policy Brief* 13, Groupe de Recherche en Appui à la Politique par la DGD et la CU, Université de Liège, Liège, http://orbi.ulg.ac.be/bitstream/2268/163420/1/policy_brief_13_Evaluation.pdf.

OECD (2014), *Engaging with the Public: Twelve Lessons from DAC Peer Reviews, OECD Development Co-operation Peer Reviews*, OECD Publishing Paris, http://dx.doi.org/10.1787/9789264226739-en.

Peeters, B et al. (2013), *Évaluation à mi-parcours, Annoncer la couleur,* Kleur Bekennen, South Research CVBA-VSO, Kessel.

Chapter 7: Belgium's humanitarian assistance

Strategic framework

Indicator: Clear political directives and strategies for resilience, response and recovery

Belgium has made enormous progress on its strategic approach to humanitarian assistance over the last four years, modernising its legal, policy and budgetary framework to allow quality, predictable funding arrangements in areas where it can clearly add value. The new framework allows for holistic programming and greater scope, including areas such as recovery and risk reduction. Belgium now needs to determine how it will make use of these new opportunities, including embedding risk into development partner country strategies. The budget is sufficient to meet Belgium's humanitarian objectives, although it will, in line with wider austerity measures, decline by 25% over the next five years. Disbursement has been an issue in the past, mostly due to administrative procedures outside DGD's control; this has led to underspending. Belgium needs to put measures in place to prevent this happening in the future.

A modernised humanitarian framework focuses on areas where Belgium can clearly add value

The legal, policy and budgetary frameworks for humanitarian assistance have been significantly modernised and improved, allowing for more predictable and flexible aid, focused on areas where Belgium can clearly add value. Belgium's administrative system and dynamic political environment require very normative legal instruments. The new Royal Decree, therefore, outlines exactly what can, and what cannot be done, but it has been carefully worded to allow flexibility and a holistic range of programming (Kingdom of Belgium, 2014). The Decree also recognises internationally accepted good practice such as the Principles and Good Practice of Humanitarian Donorship (GHD, 2003) and the Do No Harm principle.[1] The 2015 budget picks up these elements, ensuring implementation (FPS FA, 2015). Belgian NGOs were consulted in the policy-setting process, which is good practice.

Financing rules allow more holistic socio-economic recovery programming

The 2010 peer review recommended that Belgium strengthen links between relief and development (OECD, 2010). The new Royal Decree allows humanitarian funding to cover elements such as rehabilitation and socio-economic recovery, significantly increasing the scope of humanitarian programming; this is good practice. Partners confirm that Belgian funding now allows for more holistic approaches. The decree is of course very new; Belgium is encouraged to ensure that the good intentions enshrined in this document are put into practice fully.

Risk reduction could be more strategic

The new humanitarian framework also recognises the importance of risk reduction, and allows for funding to this area of work. There are some standalone projects focused on disaster preparedness, for example in Latin America. However, Belgium is still reflecting on how to take a systematic approach towards risk reduction. Incorporating risk elements in partner country strategies could be a useful first step.

Belgium is a medium size humanitarian donor, with looming budget cuts

Belgium allocates around 10% of its total ODA budget to humanitarian assistance, with USD 169.3 million disbursed in 2013, placing it firmly among the top 15 OECD/DAC donors.[2] However, fiscal consolidation measures will mean cuts to the overall budget over the next four years (Chapter 3), and this will affect the volume available for humanitarian programmes. The latest budget outlines cuts of 25%: from EUR 150 million in 2015 down to EUR 120 million in 2019 (FPS FA, 2015). In addition, the humanitarian team is no longer receiving unspent development funds.

Disbursement of the humanitarian budget was difficult in 2014: the new Royal Decree was only put in place in the middle of the year, and thus the majority of funding decisions had to be made under the old – very restrictive – 1996 decree. This, plus an early, unexpected, year-end administrative close, led to around EUR 50 million of the 2014 humanitarian budget being returned unspent to the state coffers. Belgium should ensure that future humanitarian allocation plans allow for such uncertainties, perhaps by disbursing earlier in the year, or by signing agreements with partners for rapid disbursement if administrative restrictions are re-imposed.

Effective programme design

Indicator: Programmes target the highest risk to life and livelihood

There is now a clear policy focus for the humanitarian programme, linked in to Belgium's overall strategic priorities. However, actual funding allocations – set out, and thus ring-fenced for four years, in the budget – heavily favour core funding to the multilateral system and pooled funds. This means that Belgium's focus is more on specific partnerships than on specific crises and themes. This is a useful strategy, providing excellent predictability for partners, reducing the risk of politicised decision making, and providing an efficient way to disburse, given the limited number of humanitarian staff. It also allows Belgium to place the onus for early action on partners; this is useful given its complex (and thus slow) administrative procedures.

A clear strategic focus, mostly on who, rather than what and where to fund

The 2010 peer review asked Belgium to determine its strategic niche for humanitarian assistance, based on its comparative advantage (OECD, 2010). This has been done. The new decree focuses on the Sahel, the Great Lakes area and the West Bank and Gaza Strip; clear links between these areas and Belgium's overall strategic priorities (Chapter 2) make this a good choice. The issues to fund in these crises depend on priorities on the ground, with some sectors specifically singled out.[3] Partners are approved following strict quality criteria.[4] However, in practice, Belgium has allowed itself little flexibility in targeting its funding – most of the budget (52% in 2105, rising to 67% in 2019) is already allocated to multiannual core allocations to partners and pooled funds, with only one of the pooled funds – for the DR Congo – specifically targeting the geographic area outlined in the decree. The decision to allocate funding this way is good practice, as it provides predictability for partners and insulates the programme from political influence; however it does mean that Belgium's de facto focus is actually on specific partnerships, rather than on specific crises (Figure 7.1).

Funding rapid response mechanisms helps early action

Belgium recognises that its administrative procedures are complex and time consuming, hindering a rapid response to early warnings; to get round this it allocates funding to rapid pooled mechanisms, which can make more rapid funding decisions. For example, Belgium plans to allocate EUR 1 million a year to the Red Cross Movement's Disaster Relief Emergency Fund (DREF) and EUR 15 million a year to the UN system's Central Emergency Relief Fund (CERF).

Belgium promotes beneficiary participation through partners

Ensuring the participation of affected people in the programme cycle is difficult for donors who are not present in the field. Belgium, like others, encourages its partners to seek input from affected people by checking this in the programme appraisal process, and backing it up with flexible funding to ensure that feedback is taken into account.

Figure 7.1 Belgium's humanitarian budget, planned disbursements, 2015 and 2019

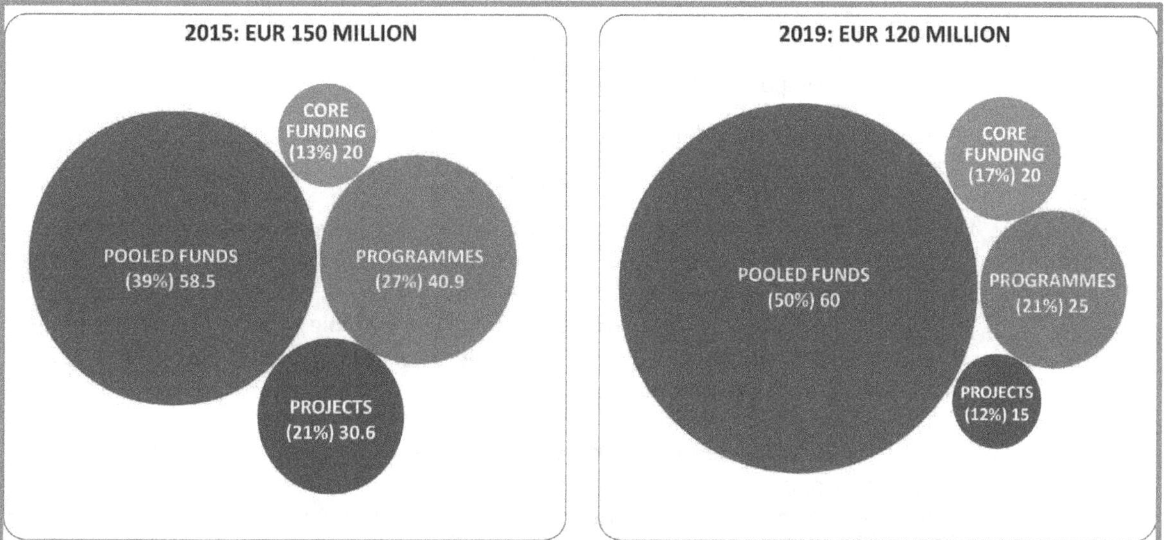

Source: Authors' compilation on the basis of *FPS FA (2015),* Budget général des dépenses 2015, *FPS Foreign Affairs, Foreign Trade and Development Cooperation, Brussels*

Effective delivery, partnerships and instruments

Indicator: Delivery modalities and partnerships help deliver quality

There are new tools to deliver on the new strategic framework. The majority of Belgium's funding will, in future, be provided through multiannual, unearmarked grants to multilateral partners and pooled funds – including for rapid response – providing both predictability and flexibility to the multilateral system. This provides the basis for quality partnerships with multilateral agencies. Unfortunately, there is not yet the same quality relationship with NGOs, who were consulted on the overall strategic approach, but are no longer engaged in strategic dialogue or programming, and have unclear guidance on how to apply for funds. Belgium might now review its strategy for engaging with NGOs. In addition, with the share of investments in pooled funding mechanisms set to rise from 39% of the budget in 2015 to 50% in 2019, Belgium might need to think more about how it approaches these types of investments – perhaps by involving itself more in pooled fund governance arrangements – to be sure it is adding value to this part of the portfolio.

New tools foster quality partnerships and funding for protracted emergencies

The 2010 peer review asked Belgium to widen its categories of eligible expenditure; Belgium has gone well beyond this in its new framework, with a majority of its humanitarian funding to be provided as multiannual, unearmarked grants to multilateral organisations and pooled funds (from 52% in 2015 to 67% by 2019; Figure 7.1).[5] Naming partners and specifying allocations in the budget helps ring-fence and protect these allocations, providing good predictability to partners. All funding decisions are made in the first quarter of each year, which should improve the timeliness of future disbursements, which has been a problem in the recent past. Funding under the project budget line can be for up to 18 months, which provides continuity. A broad range of eligible expenditure allows for holistic programming. Belgium is, however, not yet active in the governance structures of its pooled fund partners – when such structures exist. This could be a useful way for Belgium to add value to this area of the humanitarian portfolio, especially given that its investments in pooled funds will represent 39% of the total 2015 humanitarian budget, rising to 50% by 2019.

Use of pooled funds for rapid response gets around slow administrative procedures

Belgium uses three main means to support the rapid response to new or escalating crises:

- giving support to rapid response pooled funds
- giving project funding to accredited partners
- using the civil protection mechanism B-FAST.[6]

Slow administrative procedures and a difficult approval process have led Belgium to favour pooled funds, as they can intervene more quickly. Project funding has been complicated in the recent past, as it was guided by the 1996 Royal Decree, which was very restrictive. In 2014, for example, only one grant of EUR 3 million was able to be finalised. Belgium is working on new guidance for NGOs seeking to access project funding; the rapid completion of this guidance is to be encouraged.[7]

Partnerships with multilaterals are good, which is not yet the case with NGOs

The 2010 review asked Belgium to reduce the administrative burden on its partners. This is already happening for multilateral partners and funds, and the planned move towards multiannual funding for these partners is a good next step. Belgium engages actively on multilateral boards and donor support groups, feeding in information from the field and focusing on key strategic issues, although it is not yet involved in the boards of pooled funds. The picture is not quite so rosy for NGO partners, however, mostly because of a lack of clarity over the scope of dialogue between partners and the Ministry, and on the procedures for applying for funds, leading to a very unpredictable relationship. Belgium might now review when and how it engages with NGOs, both on policy and operational (funding) matters.

Belgium plays an active role in donor co-ordination

Belgium participates actively in donor co-ordination groups such as the EU's Council Working Party on Humanitarian Aid and Food Aid (COHAFA)[8] and the Good Humanitarian Donorship initiative, where it leads the work on indicators. It also has regular informal interactions with ECHO (the European Commission's Humanitarian Aid and Civil Protection department), facilitated by the two donors being based in the same city.

Organisation fit for purpose

Indicator: Systems, structures, processes and people work together effectively and efficiently

The humanitarian team is usefully plugged in to cross-government mechanisms on protracted crises and emergency situations, allowing them to influence Belgium's overall policy and operations. This has also helped increase awareness of humanitarian principles in a range of ministries. While staff numbers have been cut, the team believes it is still able to manage the humanitarian portfolio effectively, especially now that the emphasis is on large strategic partnerships rather than small grants. The workload is nevertheless high, and there is little time left for strategic reflection, or for input to thematic debates at global level.

Informal cross-government mechanisms on crises are useful

The humanitarian team participates in cross-government co-ordination mechanisms on specific crises and issues, including Syria, Mali and Niger (Chapters 4 and 5) and Ebola. Depending on the nature of the crisis, these mechanisms may include staff from the ministries of the interior, health, defence, and others. Humanitarian staff report that these mechanisms – though not formal structures – allow them to promote humanitarian considerations within Belgian policy and operations, and have also helped raise awareness of humanitarian principles across government.

Belgium has no civil-military policy

There is no civil-military policy in Belgium, and no formal structures. However, no civil military co-ordination issues were raised during this peer review.

Staff cuts mean less time to focus on policy and thematic issues

The number of humanitarian staff has been cut since the last peer review in line with broader cuts across DGD (Chapter 4). The cuts are manageable, especially now that the programme focuses on a smaller number of strategic partnerships, and less on small grants, which come with a high administrative workload. That being said, staff report less time to work on thematic issues such as the upcoming World Humanitarian Summit and issues raised at the EU. New field staff are trained in humanitarian principles. This has helped them consider humanitarian issues as a normal part of their jobs, ensuring useful field input, for example, to project approvals and at multilateral board meetings.

Results, learning and accountability

Indicator: Results are measured and communicated, and lessons learnt

The previous peer review asked Belgium to focus more on monitoring its own results and those of partners, rather than on due diligence procedures in the grant approval process. There has been some progress on this, as part of the overall management plan, but it is still not entirely clear how Belgium assesses its progress or results. For NGO grants in particular, there seems to be a focus on fiduciary risk rather than on results and learning.

Expected results are set out in DGD's management plan

The 2010 peer review asked Belgium to adopt a results-based framework to monitor its performance as a donor (OECD, 2010). In response to this recommendation, DGD's management plan contains specific humanitarian targets (Chapter 4).

There is a shift towards monitoring results, but continued focus on fiduciary risk

The previous peer review also recommended that Belgium shift its focus towards monitoring its partners' results, rather than spending time on due diligence before making funding decisions. For core contributions to multilaterals and pooled funds, Belgium accepts standard narrative and financial reports. For programme contributions, earmarked for specific themes, for example, separate reports are required, even from multilaterals. NGOs have much more onerous reporting requirements, including progress and final reports, and external audit reports on each project. This seems to suggest that Belgium is still more focused on controlling fiduciary risk, especially in NGO funding, than on measuring results.

Belgium could communicate better and fund research

While Belgium has a webpage that outlines some basic facts about the humanitarian programme, it mainly contains policy documents, and does not communicate results.[9] This seems to be a missed opportunity. Belgium's new framework allows for funding of research; this could be useful to increase knowledge in areas of strategic interest to Belgium, and is to be encouraged.

Notes

1. See: http://cdacollaborative.org/programs/do-no-harm/.
2. Source: OECD Creditor Reporting System, current prices.
3. Food security, nutrition and agriculture, as well as protection (especially of children), health, logistics and preparedness are specifically mentioned in the different documents that make up the Belgian humanitarian framework.
4. NGO partners must be accredited either by the European Union, under ECHO's (the Humanitarian Office) Framework Partnership Agreement process (see: http://dgecho-partners-helpdesk.eu/partnership/start), or by certification under the Humanitarian Accountability Partnership standard (www.hapinternational.org/what-we-do/certification.aspx). United Nations and other multilateral partners must be members of, or observers of, the Inter-Agency Standing Committee (see: www.humanitarianinfo.org/iasc/).
5. Belgium plans to provide three-year multi-annual commitments (with equal tranches each year) to its multilateral partners, and to provide two-year multi-annual commitments to its chosen pooled funds.
6. See: http://b-fast.be/fr/content/historique.
7. A vademecum has been discussed with the NGOs and is in the process of being approved.
8. See: http://ec.europa.eu/echo/fr/partnerships/relations/member-states-cohafa.
9. See: http://diplomatie.belgium.be/en/policy/development_cooperation/what_we_do/themes/humanitarian_aid/.

Bibliography

Government sources

FPS FA (2015), *Budget Général des Dépenses 2015*, FPS Foreign Affairs, Foreign Trade and Development Cooperation, Brussels

Kingdom of Belgium (2014), *Arrêté royal relatif à l'aide humanitaire*, 19 April 2014, *Moniteur Belge*, Brussels.

Other sources

Good Humanitarian Donorship (2003), The Principles and Good Practice of Humanitarian Donorship, declaration signed in Stockholm, https://www.worldhumanitariansummit.org/file/434472/download/473124.

OECD (2010), *OECD Development Assistance Peer Reviews: Belgium 2010*, OECD Publishing, Paris, http://dx.doi.org/10.1787/9789264098268-en.

Annex A: Progress since the 2010 DAC peer review recommendations

Key Issues: Development beyond aid

Recommendation 2010	Progress in implementation
Belgium is invited to develop an explicit policy statement on policy coherence for development, and promote a better understanding of this concept amongst government entities and the wider public. Identify the institutional framework and tools Belgium will use to implement and monitor the coherent use of all policy levers for development, and to report on it.	**Implemented**

Key Issues: Strategic orientations

Recommendations 2010	Progress in implementation
Belgium should definitely (a) develop a common vision of development co-operation through dialogue involving all the public actors delivering Belgian ODA; (b) a medium-term strategy should translate this vision into operational and strategic priorities for development programming.	**Implemented**
Belgium should ensure that sector and cross-cutting strategies are up to date, maximise the synergies among the various entities delivering Belgian aid, and are guided by operational good practice and oriented towards results.	**Implemented**
Belgium is encouraged to formulate a whole-of-government position for Belgium's engagement in fragile contexts which is built on good practice, links efforts to bring about peace and security with statebuilding and poverty reduction efforts, and is translated into operations.	**Partially implemented** (A whole-of-government approach has not been formulated.)

Key Issues: Aid volume, channels and allocations

Recommendations 2010	Progress in implementation
Belgium should define a medium-term budgetary plan for how it will secure increased ODA resources in light of its 0.7% ODA/GNI target beyond 2010.	**Not implemented**
Belgium should anticipate difficulties in implementing bilateral co-operation and spending plans in fragile contexts, and address this through flexible financial programming and risk strategies.	**Partially implemented** (More flexible financial programming is possible.)

Key Issues: Organisation and management

Recommendations 2010	Progress in implementation
Belgium should ensure that the mandates and the relationships among the entities delivering the aid programme in its development co-operation are clear. It should clarify the division of labour between the Policy Cell under the Minister of Development Cooperation and DGD's Policy Support Unit with regard to their respective responsibilities for development co-operation policy.	**Implemented**
Belgium should define a human resources policy for DGD that allows DGD to play its strategic role by providing for (1) more mobility between headquarters and the field, (2) a human resources plan that includes the profiles of specialists it might require, (3) provisions for accessing the expertise of development partners, and (4) a competency-based salary scale for locally recruited staff.	**Implemented**
Belgium should delegate more authority to development attachés and follow through on its plan to decentralise the formulation process for new indicative co-operation programmes.	**Partially implemented**

Key Issues: Delivery and partnerships

Recommendations 2010	Progress in implementation
Belgium should examine the programme and project approval process with a view to making it more efficient, and assess the development value of its multiple small schemes.	**Implemented**
Belgium should formulate a strategic framework which sets out a joint approach by DGD and BTC to supporting partner countries' capacity development.	**Partially implemented** (There is no joint strategic framework for DGD and BTC, but they have reviewed their approach to technical co-operation and analysing national systems.)
Belgium is invited to strengthen its analytical capacity and ability to formulate sector policy on rural development and food security, and ensure that its instruments for supporting development in the agriculture sector are co-ordinated and that their use creates synergies in the field.	**Not reviewed**

Key Issues: Results management and accountability

Recommendations 2010	Progress in implementation
Belgium is encouraged to strengthen its systems to manage for development results and its use of lessons to design new development interventions.	**Partially implemented** (DGD's results strategy has not yet been approved, so work is still in progress on implementing the recommendation.)
Belgium should incorporate lessons from evaluations into policy making, and promote an evaluation culture.	**Implemented**

Humanitarian assistance

Recommendations 2010	Progress in implementation
Belgium should implement the recommendations of the 2008 Humanitarian Assistance Evaluation, including widening the categories for eligible expenditure, shifting focus to results-based monitoring, and reducing the administrative burden on partners.	**Implemented**
The proposed revision of the 1996 Royal Decree creates an opportunity for Belgium to determine the strategic niche for Belgium's humanitarian aid, based on comparative advantage.	**Implemented**
Belgium is invited to strengthen links between relief efforts and development co-operation, and improve strategic and day-to-day co-ordination between instruments.	**Implemented**

Figure A.1 Belgium's implementation of 2010 peer review recommendations

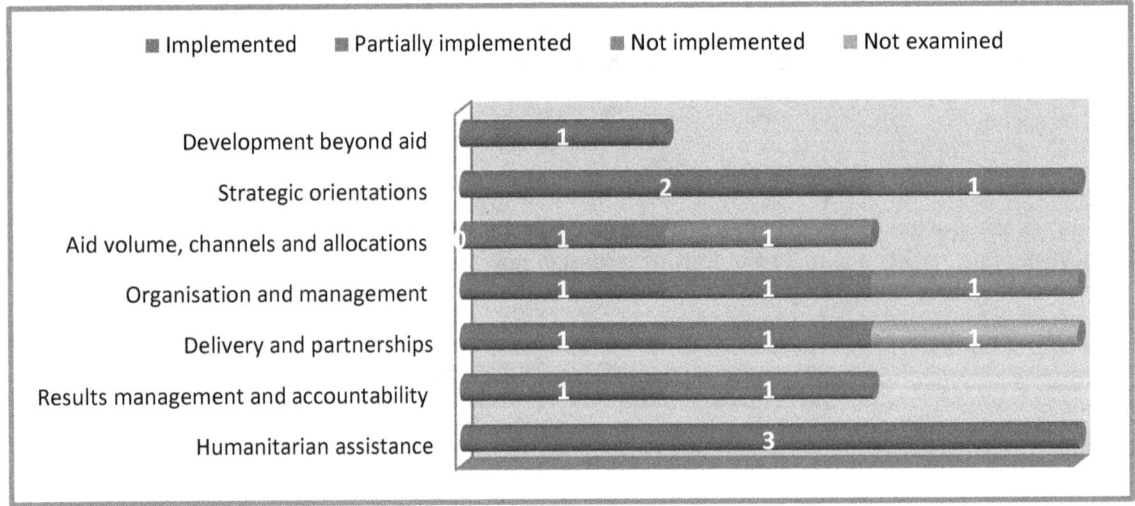

Annex B: OECD/DAC standard suite of tables

Table B.1 Total financial flows

USD million at current prices and exchange rates

Belgium	1999-2003	2004-2008	2009	2010	2011	2012	2013
							Net disbursements
Total official flows	1 271	1 861	2 700	2 989	2 793	2 370	2 376
Official development assistance	1 074	1 948	2 610	3 004	2 807	2 315	2 300
Bilateral	719	1 236	1 585	2 051	1 739	1 433	1 307
Multilateral	355	712	1 025	953	1 068	882	992
Other official flows	197	- 87	90	- 15	- 15	55	76
Bilateral	197	- 87	90	- 15	- 15	55	76
Multilateral	-	-	-	-	-	-	-
Net Private Grants	107	277	377	377	519	-	664
Private flows at market terms	756	1 364	147	4 530	-2 126	333	7 178
Bilateral: *of which*	756	1 364	147	4 530	-2 126	333	7 178
Direct investment	560	1 578	3	4 790	-2 134	-	6 397
Export credits	- 356	- 214	144	- 259	8	333	780
Multilateral	-	-	-	-	-	-	-
Total flows	2 134	3 502	3 224	7 896	1 185	2 703	10 218
for reference:							
ODA (at constant 2012 USD million)	*1 707*	*2 136*	*2 557*	*3 033*	*2 646*	*2 315*	*2 192*
ODA (as a % of GNI)	*0.42*	*0.47*	*0.55*	*0.64*	*0.54*	*0.47*	*0.45*
Total flows (as a % of GNI) (a)	*0.84*	*0.84*	*0.68*	*1.68*	*0.23*	*0.55*	*2.01*
ODA to and channelled through NGOs							
- In USD million	97	210	303	322	354	300	322
- In percentage of total net ODA	9	11	12	11	13	13	14
- DAC countries' average % of total net ODA	*8*	*8*	*7*	*8*	*9*	*13*	*13*

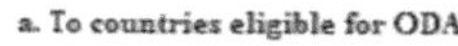
a. To countries eligible for ODA.

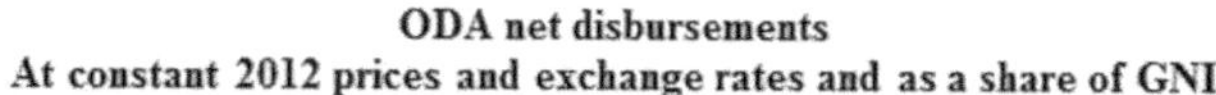
ODA net disbursements
At constant 2012 prices and exchange rates and as a share of GNI

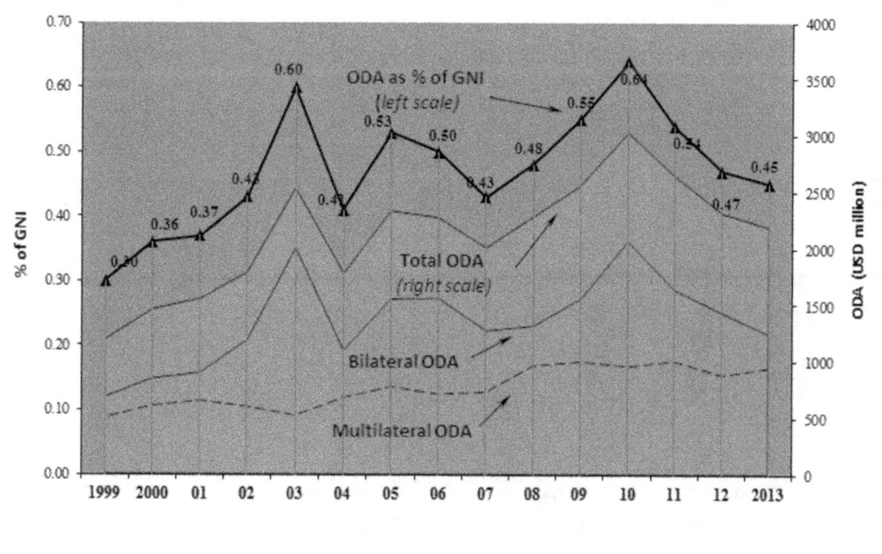

Table B.2 ODA by main categories

Disbursements

Belgium	Constant 2012 USD million					Per cent share of gross disbursements					Total DAC 2013%
	2009	2010	2011	2012	2013	2009	2010	2011	2012	2013	
Gross Bilateral ODA	**1 630**	**2 119**	**1 838**	**1 477**	**1 300**	**62**	**69**	**65**	**63**	**58**	**73**
Budget support	-	64	30	32	36	-	2	1	1	2	4
of which: General budget support	0	12	-	-	-	0	0	-	-	-	2
Core contributions & pooled prog.& funds	-	455	462	290	379	-	15	16	12	17	13
of which: Core support to national NGOs	176	187	194	186	191	7	6	7	8	9	1
Core support to international NGOs	1	3	3	16	14	0	0	0	1	1	1
Core support to PPPs	1	153	154	2	27	0	5	5	0	1	0
Project-type interventions	-	626	619	453	490	-	20	22	19	22	39
of which: Investment projects	343	151	135	98	106	13	5	5	4	5	12
Experts and other technical assistance	-	115	114	102	38	-	4	4	4	2	4
Scholarships and student costs in donor countries	-	90	93	92	91	-	3	3	4	4	2
of which: Imputed student costs	44	46	49	51	54	2	2	2	2	2	1
Debt relief grants	107	561	292	278	17	4	18	10	12	1	4
Administrative costs	93	93	94	91	89	4	3	3	4	4	4
Other in-donor expenditures	107	115	133	139	161	4	4	5	6	7	3
of which: refugees in donor countries	90	96	120	126	149						
Gross Multilateral ODA	**1 004**	**962**	**1 007**	**882**	**946**	**38**	**31**	**35**	**37**	**42**	**27**
UN agencies	138	148	159	145	140	5	5	6	6	6	4
EU institutions	579	551	494	450	472	22	18	17	19	21	8
World Bank group	153	153	177	189	187	6	5	6	8	8	6
Regional development banks	64	39	85	9	56	2	1	3	0	2	3
Other multilateral	69	71	91	88	90	3	2	3	4	4	5
Total gross ODA	**2 634**	**3 081**	**2 845**	**2 359**	**2 246**	**100**	**100**	**100**	**100**	**100**	**100**
Repayments and debt cancellation	**- 77**	**- 48**	**- 199**	**- 44**	**- 55**						
Total net ODA	**2 557**	**3 033**	**2 646**	**2 315**	**2 192**						
For reference:											
Free standing technical co-operation	*501*	*679*	*484*	*336*	*489*						
Net debt relief	*107*	*561*	*292*	*278*	*17*						

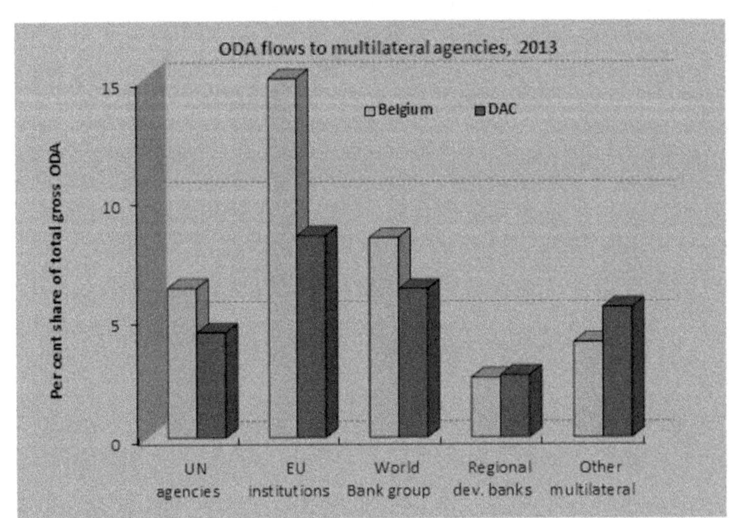

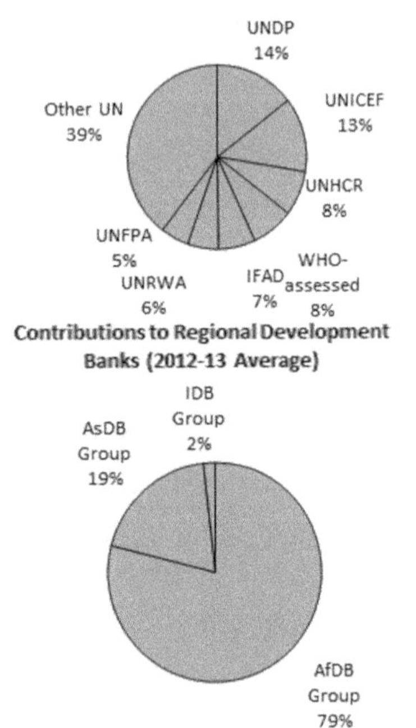

Table B.3 Bilateral ODA allocable by region and income group

Gross disbursements

Belgium	Constant 2012 USD million					Per cent share					Total DAC
	2009	2010	2011	2012	2013	2009	2010	2011	2012	2013	2013%
Africa	792	1 239	953	788	569	76	84	81	79	74	40
Sub-Saharan Africa	744	1 195	895	755	540	72	81	76	76	70	34
North Africa	38	37	49	29	25	4	2	4	3	3	4
Asia	102	87	87	76	67	10	6	7	8	9	37
South and Central Asia	42	42	40	27	18	4	3	3	3	2	24
Far East	57	42	43	46	46	5	3	4	5	6	12
America	109	114	101	91	85	11	8	9	9	11	9
North and Central America	35	48	35	28	26	3	3	3	3	3	4
South America	73	66	66	62	58	7	4	6	6	8	4
Middle East	31	30	34	37	44	3	2	3	4	6	9
Oceania	-	-	0	-	-	-	-	0	-	-	2
Europe	2	2	4	2	1	0	0	0	0	0	3
Total bilateral allocable by region	1 037	1 472	1 180	994	767	100	100	100	100	100	100
Least developed	611	1 101	849	449	481	63	77	75	47	66	45
Other low-income	35	10	22	9	19	4	1	2	1	3	4
Lower middle-income	217	233	163	421	141	22	16	14	44	19	35
Upper middle-income	112	93	93	82	85	11	6	8	9	12	16
More advanced developing countries	0	0	-	-	-	0	0	-	-	-	-
Total bilateral allocable by income	976	1 438	1 127	961	727	100	100	100	100	100	100
For reference:											
Total bilateral	1 601	2 119	1 838	1 477	1 301	*100*	*100*	*100*	*100*	*100*	*100*
of which: Unallocated by region	*563*	*647*	*658*	*483*	*534*	*35*	*31*	*36*	*33*	*41*	*25*
of which: Unallocated by income	*625*	*682*	*712*	*516*	*574*	*39*	*32*	*39*	*35*	*44*	*31*

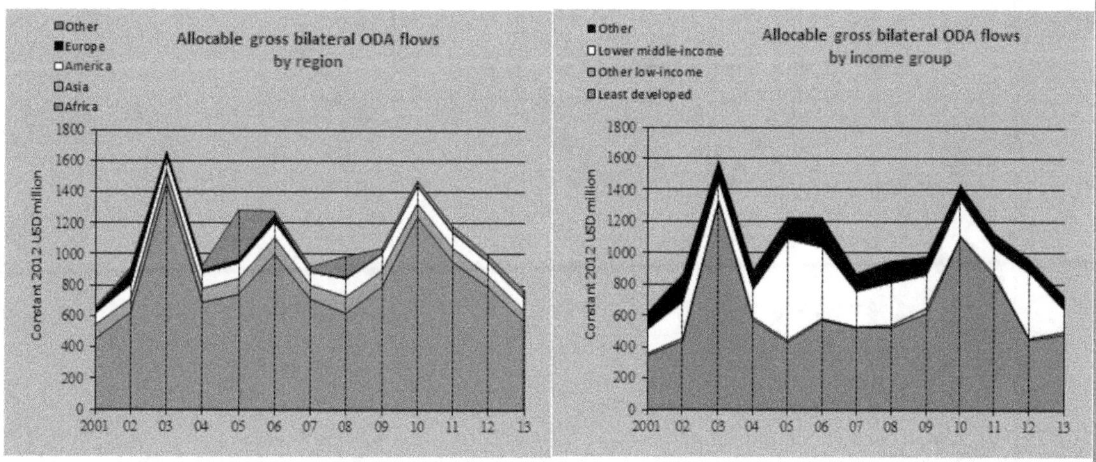

1. Each region includes regional amounts which cannot be allocated by sub-region. The sum of the sub-regional amounts may therefore fall short of the regional total.

Table B.4 Main recipients of bilateral ODA

Gross disbursements

Belgium	2002-06 average			Memo: DAC countries' average %
	Current USD million	Constant 2012 USD mln	Per cent share	
Democratic Republic of the Congo	297	385	25	
Nigeria	68	80	6	
Iraq	51	60	4	
Cameroon	32	41	3	
Tanzania	25	37	2	
Top 5 recipients	**473**	**603**	**39**	**50**
Rwanda	25	32	2	
Burundi	23	30	2	
South Africa	16	21	1	
Serbia	16	24	1	
Ecuador	16	20	1	
Top 10 recipients	**569**	**730**	**47**	**68**
Burkina Faso	16	21	1	
Viet Nam	15	20	1	
Senegal	15	19	1	
Bolivia	14	19	1	
Côte d'Ivoire	14	21	1	
Top 15 recipients	**643**	**829**	**53**	**76**
Benin	12	16	1	
Peru	12	15	1	
Morocco	12	15	1	
Niger	12	15	1	
West Bank and Gaza Strip	11	14	1	
Top 20 recipients	**702**	**905**	**58**	**80**
Total (122 recipients)	900	1 157	75	
Unallocated	307	398	25	5
Total bilateral gross	**1 207**	**1 555**	**100**	**100**

	2007-11 average			Memo: DAC countries' average %
	Current USD million	Constant 2012 USD mln	Per cent share	
Democratic Republic of the Congo	310	306	18	
Rwanda	68	66	4	
Burundi	52	51	3	
Togo	32	31	2	
Mozambique	28	27	2	
Top 5 recipients	**490**	**482**	**29**	**37**
West Bank and Gaza Strip	25	25	1	
Niger	25	24	1	
Cameroon	25	25	1	
Benin	24	24	1	
Viet Nam	24	23	1	
Top 10 recipients	**613**	**604**	**36**	**51**
Tanzania	22	21	1	
Iraq	21	21	1	
Senegal	21	21	1	
Peru	21	21	1	
Morocco	21	21	1	
Top 15 recipients	**720**	**708**	**42**	**55**
Bolivia	20	20	1	
Mali	20	20	1	
Uganda	19	19	1	
South Africa	17	17	1	
Ghana	17	16	1	
Top 20 recipients	**814**	**800**	**48**	**58**
Total (121 recipients)	1 090	1 072	64	
Unallocated	613	601	36	24
Total bilateral gross	**1 703**	**1 673**	**100**	**100**

	2012-13 average			Memo: DAC countries average %
	Current USD million	Constant 2012 USD mln	Per cent share	
Democratic Republic of the Congo	138	135	10	
Côte d'Ivoire	138	138	10	
Burundi	61	60	4	
Rwanda	51	49	4	
West Bank and Gaza Strip	33	33	2	
Top 5 recipients	**421**	**414**	**30**	**36**
Viet Nam	29	28	2	
Benin	25	25	2	
Mali	23	23	2	
Niger	21	21	2	
Mozambique	21	21	2	
Top 10 recipients	**541**	**531**	**38**	**50**
Senegal	21	20	1	
Tanzania	19	19	1	
South Africa	19	18	1	
Uganda	19	18	1	
Peru	17	17	1	
Top 15 recipients	**636**	**624**	**45**	**57**
Ecuador	16	16	1	
Morocco	16	16	1	
Bolivia	15	15	1	
Malawi	13	13	1	
Kenya	13	12	1	
Top 20 recipients	**709**	**695**	**50**	**61**
Total (103 recipients)	862	844	61	
Unallocated	559	545	39	28
Total bilateral gross	**1 421**	**1 389**	**100**	**100**

Table B.5 Bilateral ODA by major purposes at constant prices and exchange rates

Commitments - Two-year average

Belgium	2002-2006 average		2007-11 average		2012-13 average		2012-13
	2012 USD million	Per cent	2012 USD million	Per cent	2012 USD million	Per cent	Total DAC per cent
Social infrastructure & services	**497**	**34**	**669**	**40**	**463**	**37**	**39**
Education	155	10	217	13	179	14	8
of which: basic education	18	1	18	1	29	2	2
Health	94	6	167	10	115	9	6
of which: basic health	57	4	83	5	52	4	4
Population & reproductive health	25	2	18	1	12	1	7
Water supply & sanitation	38	3	65	4	28	2	5
Government & civil society	122	8	153	9	88	7	12
of which: Conflict, peace & security	7	0	26	2	9	1	2
Other social infrastructure & services	63	4	49	3	41	3	2
Economic infrastructure & services	**89**	**6**	**199**	**12**	**45**	**4**	**18**
Transport & storage	23	2	42	2	10	1	8
Communications	6	0	4	0	4	0	0
Energy	5	0	31	2	16	1	6
Banking & financial services	53	4	120	7	13	1	2
Business & other services	2	0	3	0	1	0	1
Production sectors	**82**	**6**	**171**	**10**	**120**	**9**	**7**
Agriculture, forestry & fishing	68	5	133	8	108	9	5
Industry, mining & construction	12	1	28	2	5	0	1
Trade & tourism	2	0	10	1	7	1	1
Multisector	**62**	**4**	**104**	**6**	**150**	**12**	**9**
Commodity and programme aid	**28**	**2**	**13**	**1**	**0**	**0**	**4**
Action relating to debt	**532**	**36**	**219**	**13**	**145**	**11**	**3**
Humanitarian aid	**68**	**5**	**121**	**7**	**118**	**9**	**9**
Administrative costs of donors	**62**	**4**	**81**	**5**	**90**	**7**	**6**
Refugees in donor countries	**63**	**4**	**96**	**6**	**137**	**11**	**4**
Total bilateral allocable	1 482	100	1 673	100	1 267	100	100
For reference:							
Total bilateral	*1 552*	*71*	*1 778*	*64*	*1 347*	*55*	*74*
of which: Unallocated	*70*	*3*	*105*	*4*	*79*	*3*	*1*
Total multilateral	*645*	*29*	*983*	*36*	*1 093*	*45*	*26*
Total ODA	***2 197***	***100***	***2 762***	***100***	***2 440***	***100***	***100***

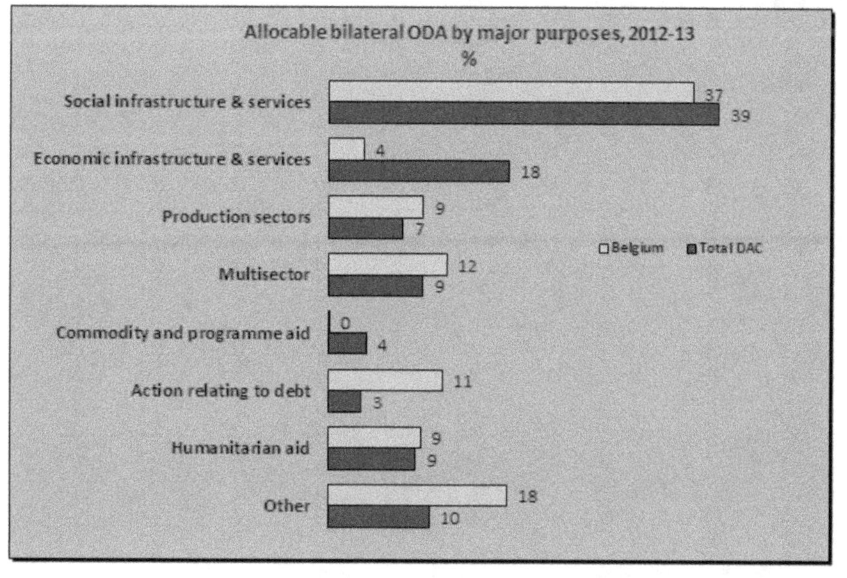

Table B.6 Comparative aid performance

Net disbursements

	Official development assistance			Grant element of ODA (commitments)	Share of multilateral aid				ODA to LDCs Bilateral and through multilateral agencies	
	2013		2007-08 to 2012-13 Average annual % change in real terms	2013	2013				2013	
					% of ODA		% of GNI			
	USD million	% of GNI		% (a)	(b)	(c)	(b)	(c)	% of ODA	% of GNI
Australia	4 846	0.33	6.0	99.9	14.0		0.05		27.6	0.09
Austria	1 171	0.27	-8.6	100.0	53.6	28.1	0.15	0.08	29.2	0.08
Belgium	2 300	0.45	1.0	99.8	43.2	21.6	0.20	0.10	35.4	0.16
Canada	4 947	0.27	0.9	100.0	29.0		0.08		37.4	0.10
Czech Republic	211	0.11	0.5	100.0	73.0	16.9	0.08	0.02	24.8	0.03
Denmark	2 927	0.85	0.2	100.0	26.8	17.9	0.23	0.15	31.6	0.27
Finland	1 435	0.54	4.6	100.0	42.7	28.9	0.23	0.15	35.5	0.19
France	11 342	0.41	2.6	84.4	40.0	20.0	0.16	0.08	30.4	0.12
Germany	14 228	0.38	0.9	86.9	33.6	15.2	0.13	0.06	23.7	0.09
Greece	239	0.10	-13.4	100.0	81.8	6.5	0.08	0.01	18.7	0.02
Iceland	35	0.25	-5.2	100.0	15.8		0.04		46.0	0.12
Ireland	846	0.46	-5.7	100.0	35.5	20.0	0.16	0.09	50.4	0.23
Italy	3 407	0.17	-7.0	99.8	75.0	27.5	0.12	0.05	28.1	0.05
Japan	11 582	0.23	2.1	89.1	25.6		0.06		60.5	0.14
Korea	1 755	0.13	16.7	95.1	25.4		0.03		40.6	0.05
Luxembourg	429	1.00	-0.9	100.0	30.4	21.5	0.30	0.22	37.9	0.38
Netherlands	5 435	0.67	-3.2	100.0	32.9	21.0	0.22	0.14	25.1	0.17
New Zealand	457	0.26	1.6	100.0	23.3		0.06		32.4	0.09
Norway	5 581	1.07	2.9	100.0	22.7		0.24		27.6	0.30
Poland	472	0.10	5.7	..	74.4	6.1	0.07	0.01	26.5	0.03
Portugal	488	0.23	0.6	87.7	38.0	5.8	0.09	0.01	29.3	0.07
Slovak Republic	86	0.09	0.1	100.0	81.2	12.1	0.08	0.01	24.4	0.02
Slovenia	62	0.13	0.1	100.0	66.5	12.7	0.09	0.02	17.5	0.02
Spain	2 375	0.17	-17.2	100.0	60.2	16.7	0.10	0.03	18.9	0.03
Sweden	5 827	1.01	2.3	100.0	32.8	26.4	0.33	0.27	31.0	0.31
Switzerland	3 197	0.47	6.1	100.0	21.6		0.10		25.9	0.12
United Kingdom	17 920	0.71	9.8	100.0	41.2	30.5	0.29	0.22	34.6	0.24
United States	30 879	0.18	3.5	100.0	14.6		0.03		33.1	0.06
Total DAC	134 481	0.30	2.0	95.1	30.4		0.09		33.3	0.10
Memo: Average country effo		0.39								

Notes:

a. Excluding debt reorganisation.

b. Including EU institutions.

c. Excluding EU institutions.

.. Data not available.

Figure B.1 - Net ODA from DAC countries in 2013

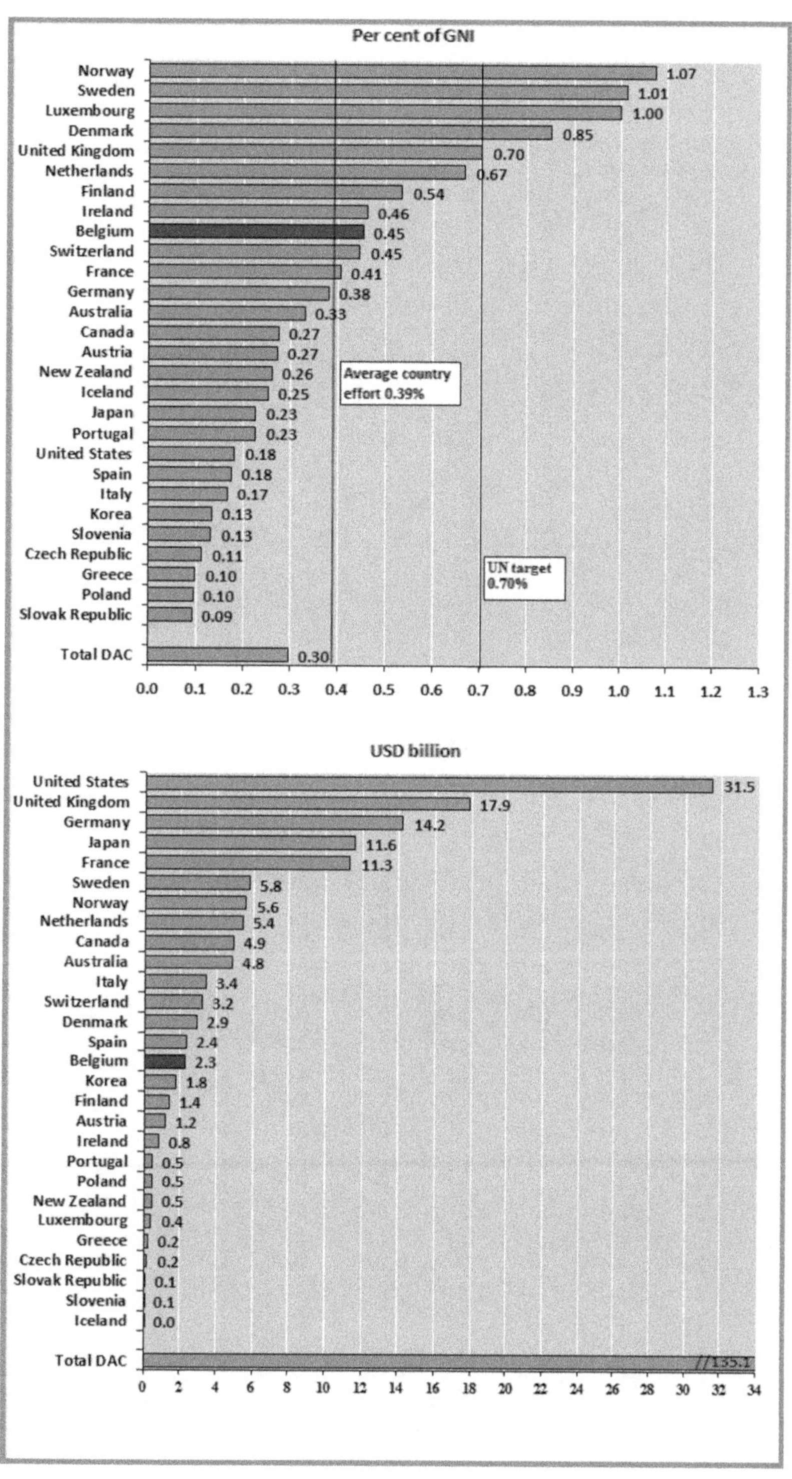

Annex C: Field visit to Rwanda

As part of the peer review of Belgium, a team of examiners from Finland and Italy and the OECD secretariat visited Rwanda in late January 2015. The team met with Belgium's Head of Cooperation in the Embassy and BTC's resident representative and their teams; Rwandan officials at the Ministry of Economy and Finance and in line ministries; parliamentarians; other bilateral and multilateral partners; and representatives of Belgian and Rwandan civil society organisations.

Towards a comprehensive Belgian development effort

Rwanda is a key partner for Belgium

There has been impressive development progress in Rwanda since the 1994 genocide. While it remains a very poor country with high levels of multidimensional poverty,[1] between 1980 and 2013 Rwanda's Human Development Index increased from 0.291 to 0.506, an average annual increase of about 1.69%. Rwanda is now consolidating gains in social welfare and accelerating growth. Its objective is to achieve middle-income status by 2020, while ensuring that advances are broadly shared. The recent setback in economic growth – partially due to the suspension of budget support disbursements in 2012 (Box C.1) – highlights how much the country still relies on external support to finance strategic public investments.

Since gaining independence in 1962, Rwanda has been one of Belgium's most important partner countries[2] due to the historical ties between the two countries. Belgium is recognised as a key player by the development community in the region. Thanks to its deep knowledge of the country and of the Great Lakes region, its long-term commitment, its presence at the local and national level and its involvement in political dialogue, Belgium is in a position to make a difference in Rwanda. Nevertheless the shared history makes the relationship very complex.

Co-ordination among the Belgian embassies in the Great Lakes region is limited

Regional integration is also a core priority for the government of Rwanda, as the Democratic Republic of the Congo and Burundi account for 30% of Rwanda's total exports.

Belgium is making a considerable effort in headquarters to co-ordinate the government's diplomatic, development and defence policy in the Great Lakes region, and the Belgian embassy in Rwanda provides feedback to aid co-ordination by headquarters. For example, while the embassy interacts with the operations of the Trade Mark East Africa project in Rwanda – which is part financed by Belgium – funding decisions are taken by headquarters. Given the importance of these regional considerations and their impact on Rwanda, Belgium could address these issues more strategically within the country programme, for example. In addition, there is little co-ordination or experience sharing among the three Belgian embassies in Burundi, Democratic Republic of Congo and Rwanda.

Belgium is exploring innovative ways to engage with the private sector

Belgium's approach in Rwanda aims to go beyond aid by using ODA as a trigger to develop the local private sector and attract Belgian companies. In addition to the loans provided by BIO to local companies, the embassy helps organise economic and trade missions to connect investors from both countries. The embassy is also working on adapting Belgium's local private sector strategy to the Rwandan context. However, these efforts to use ODA as a catalyst could be weakened by the fact that the Indicative Cooperation Programme (ICP) focuses solely on government-to-government ODA. Current efforts to improve co-ordination between BIO, the embassy and headquarters, along with the move towards an integrated programme, could improve on this situation.

C.2 Belgium's policies, strategies and aid allocation

Belgium responds to Rwanda's development needs

Belgium's engagement in Rwanda is framed by an ICP that is renewed every five years. The latest one, from 2011 to 2014, reflects Belgium's more concentrated sector focus – down from four to three (health, energy and decentralisation; see below) – as well as Rwanda's preferences for the division of labour between development partners. Indeed, Rwanda selects the sectors in which each development provider can engage. Within the sectors selected by Rwanda, Belgium's interventions are identified through dialogue with the Ministry of Finance and Economy and line ministries, which helps ensure that it responds to needs. Belgium also tries to involve the Rwandan population in discussions about its development priorities in Rwanda in order to make the policies more sustainable.

However, more reflection is needed – in consultation with relevant stakeholders, including civil society – on how Belgium can best work to support inclusive and sustainable economic growth and human rights-based approaches in this framework. Moreover, mainstreaming gender equality and environmental sustainability into Belgium's development co-operation has proved difficult for the embassy and BTC. Mainstreaming cross-cutting issues does not appear to be a strategic priority and there is limited guidance on how to do this in a pragmatic and effective way.

About 40% of Rwanda's national budget is financed by ODA

Rwanda is relatively aid dependent, with ODA contributing to 14.7% of its gross national income in 2013. The share of the national budget financed by ODA has declined significantly from about 80% over a decade ago to about 40% in 2013. In terms of volume, Rwanda received over USD 1 billion in 2013, an increase after a sharp decline in 2012 when development partners stopped providing general budget support for political reasons (Table C.1). In 2013 general budget support represented 1.2% of Rwanda's GDP, or 3.5% of the national budget (AfDB, OECD, UNDP, 2014).

Table C.1 Net ODA to Rwanda, 2009-13, USD million

	2009	2010	2011	2012	2013
All donors	961	1 069	1 235	879	1 075
Bilateral donors	538	571	582	425	565

Source: DAC CRS

Box C.1 Rwanda: a good example of the Busan principles in action

Rwanda is a developing country which has delivered a strong performance in implementing aid effectiveness principles, especially thanks to its strong government leadership. Its clear national development vision is detailed in the Economic Development and Poverty Reduction Strategy.[3] Its public financial management system is in good shape and it manages a well-structured platform for donor co-ordination and aid management.

There is also a solid framework for mutual accountability in Rwanda. Indeed, Rwanda's latest development strategy, approved in 2013, comes with a results and policy matrix, a common performance assessment framework and a development partner assessment framework that support the government's ability to assess performance and organise the division of labour among donors accordingly. The Development Partners Retreat, a senior-level two-day retreat aiming at bringing together stakeholders in Rwanda's development, is an important occasion to discuss progress in implementing the second Economic Development and Poverty Reduction Strategy and key sector policies.

The sector working groups, of which there are currently 15, provide an opportunity for co-ordination and discussion on technical and strategic matters between the government and the development partners. However, the latter regret the void left by the Budget Support Harmonisation Group in terms of both a joint political dialogue on economic and governance issues, and a common framework for performance evaluation. Now there is only a bilateral general policy dialogue, which reduces the scope for co-ordination.

Belgium could strengthen synergies among its partners around shared objectives

In 2012-13, Belgium was the sixth largest donor in Rwanda and third among bilateral partners, allocating USD 51 million, or 4.7% of total net ODA.[4]

Belgium's 2011-14 Indicative Cooperation Programme is mainly focused on the health and energy sectors – with a commitment of EUR 55 million over 4 years for each sector – and decentralisation, with a commitment of EUR 28 million to support Rwanda's Decentralisation Implementation Plan. It is also worth noting that five major existing projects are still being implemented, including in education and agriculture, increasing the number of sectors where Belgium is involved.

Belgium is equipped with a good mix of aid instruments to match the needs and capacity of its partner. In Rwanda, Belgium is one of the few donors still active in sector budget support in health, and in education through delegated co-operation. In addition, Belgium supports development in Rwanda through a range of channels and partners, including BIO, Belgian and local NGOs, universities, research institutions, regional banks etc. In light of this and the efforts made by the embassy to engage more with BIO and the local private sector, implementing an "integrated programme" approach could be useful to help co-ordinate the various partners and instruments around shared objectives.

Programming procedures hinder Belgium's capacity to adapt to rapidly changing needs

BTC and the partner government have been faced with delays of up to three years in identifying projects and in the signing of programmes and projects. In September 2014, barely 12% of the 2011-2014 ICP budget had been spent. These delays are caused by the specific context in Rwanda (a rapidly growing economy and evolving needs) and the management procedures for programme cycles. In terms of the latter, the main challenges faced by both the embassy and BTC include :

- the duration of formulation and the time lapse between formulation and implementation stages, as well as very detailed formulation and technical and financial files (Chapter 5)

- the rigid budgeting of the ICP involving individual projects/programmes rather than an overall envelope.

The fourth management contract for BTC partly addresses the first challenge by involving the agency more right from the identification phase and making it possible to hire the technical assistance and develop the baseline for each project earlier in the process. It is unclear how these changes will improve Belgium's ability to adapt to the evolving context though.

Belgium is committed to ownership and alignment

Belgium is delivering on its commitment to effective development co-operation, as defined in Busan. In addition to being actively engaged in harmonised approaches (e.g. disbursing EUR 9 million in budget support to the health sector in 2013-2014), it respects and encourages the strong leadership of the government and abides by its division of labour. For example, Belgium co-chairs two challenging sector working groups which are high priorities for the government and this co-management ensures that projects are embedded within line ministries. However, there still is a risk that the investments made to build capacity within the ministries will be lost when the project ends. The evolution towards greater national execution of projects a good way of reinforcing ownership and reducing transaction costs.

DGD headquarters encourages the embassy to take an active role in donor co-ordination by co-chairing sector working groups, for example. While the embassy is strongly committed to this involvement and is making a difference in the sectors it co-ordinates, these efforts are challenging to sustain. They resulted in an increased budget for multi-donor consultation in 2015. Moreover, embassy staff have limited sector expertise and policy dialogue relies heavily on BTC experts and technical assistants. While the study fund is a pragmatic tool to build up evidence and create shared analysis that can be used by Belgium and development partners to improve implementation, it is limited.

Belgium assesses strategic risks and seeks to mitigate them

Belgium dedicates time and resources to identifying, assessing and managing risks. In drawing up a new country programme, the embassy prepares a basic assessment of the country ("*note de base*") including chapters on risks, factors of fragility and risks of using national systems in projects and programmes. The embassy is also responsible for preparing a country note that describes the social, economic, and political institutions in the country, assesses the security situation and discusses possible trends. At project level, BTC identifies, assesses and manages risks with a clear action plan on how to mitigate them.

Consultation with Belgian NGOs could be more systematic

The embassy meets regularly with Belgian NGOs, which enables a good exchange of information. A more institutionalised and systematic approach to consulting with the NGOs could help to find synergies. CSOs questioned whether the planned joint country context analysis was the right tool for reinforcing complementarities and synergies among Belgian actors in Rwanda.

Organisation and management

Good co-ordination between the embassy and BTC ensures a strategic division of labour

Good collaboration and frequent communication between the embassy and BTC in Rwanda ensure a strategic division of labour, enhancing synergies and pragmatic ways of working. Together, the embassy and BTC give an image of Belgian co-operation built on the added value of the two actors. In addition to daily informal co-ordination, BTC is invited to the embassy's weekly co-ordination meeting and provides technical support and information from the field to feed the sector dialogue. Quarterly meetings are also organised to discuss the implementation of BTC's programmes.

Frequent co-ordination between BTC headquarters and the country representation is facilitated by "country teams" and modern communication technologies as well as BTC's operational plan that translates the agency business plan to the country level. Detailed guidance on the whole project cycle management gives BTC staff clear directions which facilitate their day-to-day work. Communication among the embassy, headquarters and other embassies in the region seems less developed, however.

Human resources are stretched in the embassy

Belgium has a dynamic team in Rwanda strongly committed to achieving the objectives of the programme and capitalising on local expertise. It faces a challenge in matching human resources to key priorities, however, which risks undermining capacity to deliver on objectives and to respond to field imperatives.

In the embassy, budgetary restrictions prevent staff training and limit the ability to find replacements in cases of long-term leave. In BTC, a training budget of EUR 250 per staff member means that all training has to been done locally. However, extra budget resources are available from headquarters. Despite a clear human resource policy for hiring local staff, the lack of clear vision for staff development might affect BTC's ability to retain them in the long term. Due to the importance of the Great Lake regions for Belgium, developing training sessions at the regional level could be both a strategic and efficient solution for staff development.

Partnerships, results and accountability

Belgium is a dynamic and much-valued partner

Belgium is recognised as a key player that can make a difference in Rwanda. Its comparative advantage stems from its deep knowledge of the country and the Great Lakes region, its long-term commitment and its presence at the local and national level.

Partners in the government and bilateral and multilateral organisations view Belgium – both the embassy and BTC – as an open, dynamic, pragmatic actor that finds constructive ways of engaging with them. Belgium engages with the government and development partners at political and technical levels in its focus sectors. They value its participatory and consultative approaches to identifying programmes and projects.

Belgium does not have a strategic vision for capacity development

Belgium is strongly involved in capacity building in Rwanda. Having a clear vision and strategic framework would help Belgium drive this work forward through the Capacity Building Coordination Forum which it co-chairs. Such a framework could also clarify the role of Belgian technical assistants in building sustainable capacity in a low capacity environment.

Results management takes place at project level

Belgium has developed a strong results-based managerial approach to interventions. For each project implemented by BTC, the agency conducts a constructive dialogue with its partners on results, including on objectives, measurement and performance. There is a risk that a detailed monitoring framework assessing outputs rather than outcomes could overlook Belgium's contribution to development in Rwanda.

Recommendations made by external and internal reviews of interventions are taken on board. However, as the mechanism for conducting external reviews is extremely formalised, it does not promote Rwanda's engagement or its efforts in the area. By engaging the partner in project evaluations and mid-term reviews, Belgium could reinforce mutual accountability and build local capacities. Moreover, it is unclear how the more general and strategic studies conducted by headquarters are used as instruments for knowledge management.

Notes

1. In 2010 (the most recent survey data available for estimating multidimensional poverty index figures for Rwanda), 69% of the population lived in multidimensional poverty while an additional 19.4% were vulnerable to multiple deprivations (http://hdr.undp.org/sites/all/themes/hdr_theme/country-notes/RWA.pdf).

2. In 2013, Rwanda was the fourth largest recipient of Belgian ODA.

3. The second strategy, approved in 2013, focuses on developing the private sector, increasing exports, urbanisation and rural development, agriculture productivity, creating jobs especially for young people and improving efficiency in service delivery in both the public and private sectors.

4. According to OECD data: https://public.Table.com/views/AidAtAGlance_Recipients/Recipients?:embed=n&:showTabs=y&:display_count=no?&:showVizHome=no#1.

Bibliography

Government sources

BTC (2014), "Programme de coopération avec le Rwanda, Rapport de suivi 2014", unpublished document, Belgian Technical Cooperation, Brussels.

BTC (2013a), *Évaluation finale conjointe du programme d'adduction d'eau potable et d'assainissement dans la Province du Sud (PEPAPS),* final report by Agrer for BTC, Brussels.

BTC (2013b), "Results report 2013 PAREF-BE2 – Rwa0907011: Support program for the forest sector in Rwanda", unpublished document, BTC, Brussels.

BTC (2013c), "Results report 2013, programme support to the SPATII: Market oriented advisory services and quality seed", unpublished document, BTC, Brussels.

BTC (2012), *Évaluation à mi-parcours du programme d'appui institutionnel au Ministère de la Santé - phase IV (MINISANTÉ IV),* Final report by HERA for BTC, Brussels.

FPS FA (2011), *Cooperation between Belgium and Rwanda, Indicative Cooperation Programme 2011-2014,* FPS Foreign Affairs, Trade and Development Cooperation, Brussels.

Joint Commission (2013), *Report on Government of Rwanda – Kingdom of Belgium Country Portfolio Performance Review Meeting*, 12 December 2013, Kigali.

Other sources

The World Bank (2015), Rwanda Overview, http://www.worldbank.org/en/country/rwanda/overview#1.

AfDB, OECD, UNDP (2014), "Rwanda", in *African Economic Outlook 2014: Global Value Chains and Africa's Industrialisation,* OECD Publishing, Paris, http://dx.doi.org/10.1787/aeo-2014-51-en.

Republic of Rwanda (2013), *"Shaping Our Development", Economic Development and Poverty Reduction Strategy 2013-2018,* Kigali.

UNDP (2014), *"Sustaining Human Progress: Reducing Vulnerabilities and Building Resilience", Explanatory note on the 2014 Human Development Report composite indices, Human Development Report 2014,* UNDP, New York.

Annex D: Organisational structure

Organisation chart of the FPS Foreign Affairs, Foreign Trade and Development Cooperation

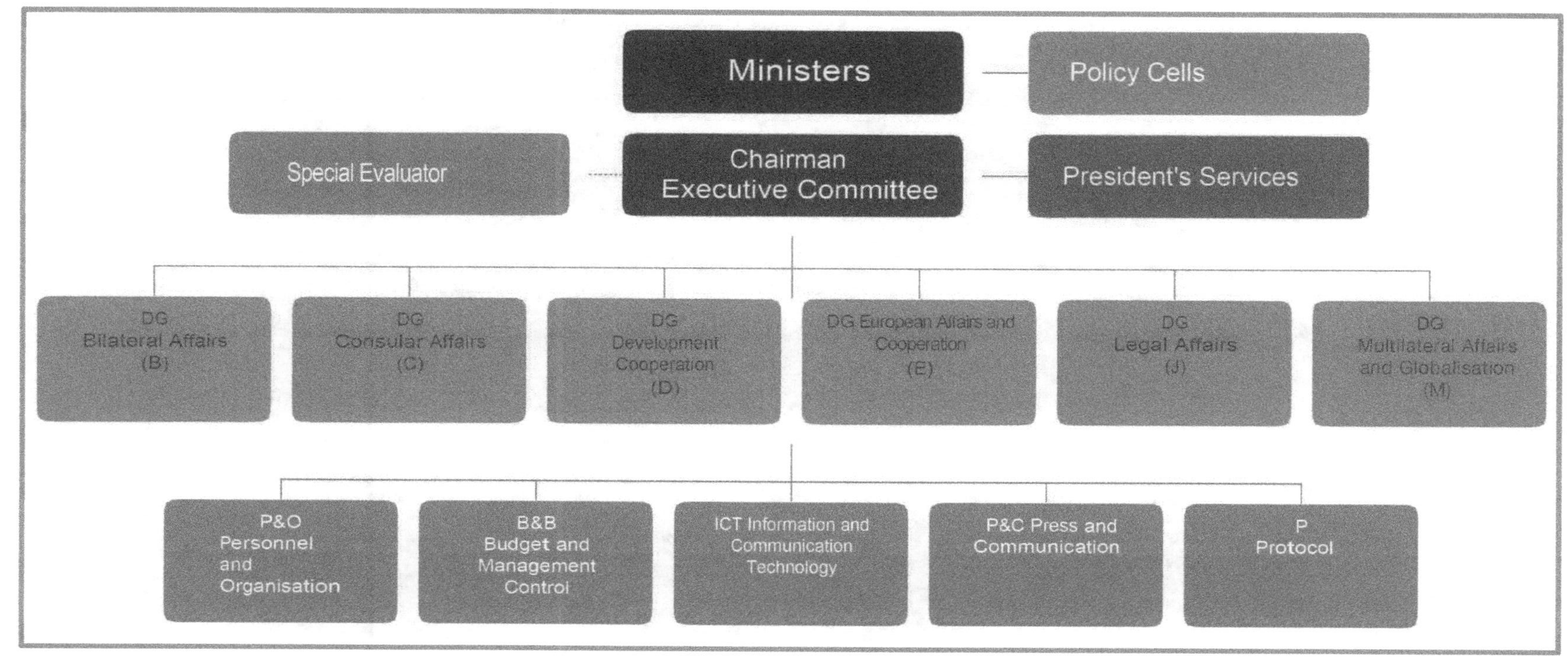

Organisation chart of the Directorate-General for Development Cooperation and Humanitarian Aid

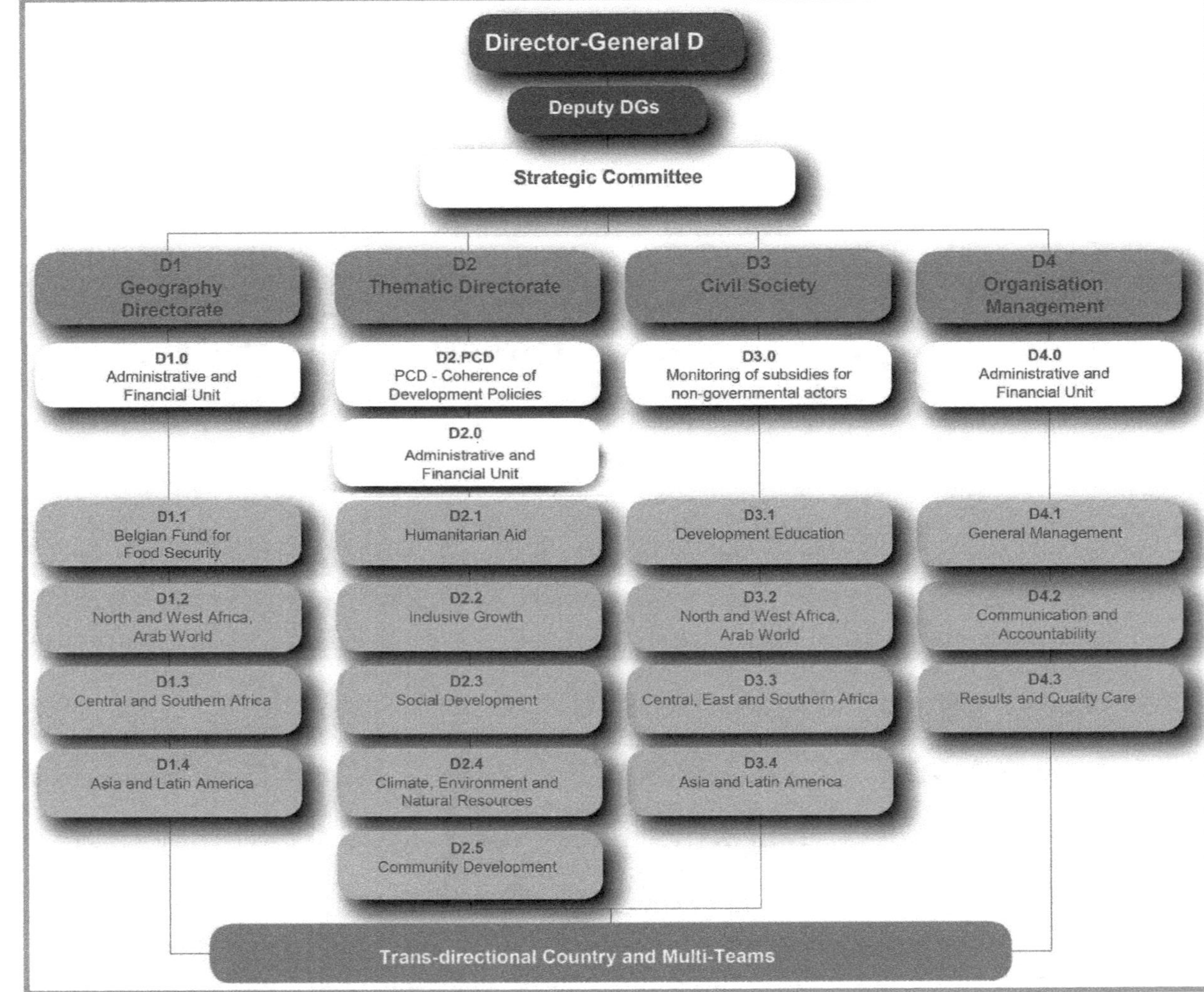

ORGANISATION FOR ECONOMIC CO-OPERATION AND DEVELOPMENT

The OECD is a unique forum where governments work together to address the economic, social and environmental challenges of globalisation. The OECD is also at the forefront of efforts to understand and to help governments respond to new developments and concerns, such as corporate governance, the information economy and the challenges of an ageing population. The Organisation provides a setting where governments can compare policy experiences, seek answers to common problems, identify good practice and work to co-ordinate domestic and international policies.

The OECD member countries are: Australia, Austria, Belgium, Canada, Chile, the Czech Republic, Denmark, Estonia, Finland, France, Germany, Greece, Hungary, Iceland, Ireland, Israel, Italy, Japan, Korea, Luxembourg, Mexico, the Netherlands, New Zealand, Norway, Poland, Portugal, the Slovak Republic, Slovenia, Spain, Sweden, Switzerland, Turkey, the United Kingdom and the United States. The European Union takes part in the work of the OECD.

OECD Publishing disseminates widely the results of the Organisation's statistics gathering and research on economic, social and environmental issues, as well as the conventions, guidelines and standards agreed by its members.

DEVELOPMENT ASSISTANCE COMMITTEE

To achieve its aims, the OECD has set up a number of specialised committees. One of these is the Development Assistance Committee (DAC), whose mandate is to promote development co-operation and other policies so as to contribute to sustainable development - including pro-poor economic growth, poverty reduction and the improvement of living standards in developing countries - and to a future in which no country will depend on aid. To this end, the DAC has grouped the world's main donors, defining and monitoring global standards in key areas of development.

The members of the DAC are Australia, Austria, Belgium, Canada, the Czech Republic, Denmark, the European Union, Finland, France, Germany, Greece, Iceland, Ireland, Italy, Japan, Korea, Luxembourg, the Netherlands, New Zealand, Norway, Poland, Portugal, the Slovak Republic, Slovenia, Spain, Sweden, Switzerland, the United Kingdom and the United States.

The DAC issues guidelines and reference documents in the DAC Guidelines and Reference Series toinform and assist members in the conduct of their development co-operation programmes.

OECD PUBLISHING, 2, rue André-Pascal, 75775 PARIS CEDEX 16
(43 2015 07 1 P) ISBN 978-92-64-23985-2 – 2015

www.ingramcontent.com/pod-product-compliance
Lightning Source LLC
LaVergne TN
LVHW080929120826
845149LV00018B/1745

* 9 7 8 9 2 6 4 2 3 9 8 5 2 *